A LIFE LESS LONELY

What we can all do to lead more connected, kinder lives

In memory of Jo Cox

A LIFE LESS LONELY

*What we can all do to lead more
connected, kinder lives*

NICK DUERDEN

GREEN TREE
LONDON · OXFORD · NEW YORK · NEW DELHI · SYDNEY

GREEN TREE
Bloomsbury Publishing Plc
50 Bedford Square, London, WC1B 3DP, UK

BLOOMSBURY, GREEN TREE and the Green Tree logo are trademarks of
Bloomsbury Publishing Plc

First published in Great Britain 2018

A catalogue record for this book is available from the British Library

Library of Congress Cataloguing-in-Publication data has been applied for

ISBN: TPB: 978-1-4729-5778-8; eBook: 978-1-4729-5779-5

2 4 6 8 10 9 7 5 3 1

Typeset in Joanna MT Pro by Deanta Global Publishing Services, Chennai, India
Printed and bound in Great Britain by CPI Group (UK) Ltd. Croydon, CR0 4YY

To find out more about our authors and books visit www.bloomsbury.com and
sign up for our newsletters

Contents

Introduction

So, here's the dilemma: how do you write a book on loneliness? How best to even attempt to tackle an often immersive condition that very likely everyone has some experience of, but one that precious few have spoken up about until very recently? What is, precisely, the most effective way to go about highlighting how we should all be dealing with it, individually and communally, attempting to overcome it, leave it behind and perhaps even – best case scenario – avoid falling prey to it in the first place?

Loneliness is that most amorphous thing. It's more tangible than depression but far less easy to explain. You cannot medicate for loneliness (although certain nationalities do try), but for many it is increasingly difficult to escape. It has been called the silent scourge, the prevailing stigma of the twenty-first century. Its dictionary definition has an enviable succinctness to it: 'a subjective, unwelcome feeling of lack, or loss, of companionship, which happens when we have a mismatch between the quantity and quality of social relationships that we have, and those we want'.

It is in that clause we find the often un-navigable gulf: *the quantity and quality of social relationships that we have, and those we want.* If there are certain sentences that resonate off the page more than others, this is one of them. We all know people, but do we know the right people? Are our friends the best friends for us, or merely acquaintances with whom we never fully connect? And if so, how on earth do we meet better ones?

Loneliness is something that can affect anyone and everyone, irrespective of age, race or class. From the bullied child to the new mother, from the pensioner who has outlived friends and family members to teenagers whose primary grasp on social life is filtered through the glow of a mobile phone, its tentacles are far-reaching and rapacious: research suggests that one in ten GP appointments today are being booked simply because people crave the social interaction they currently lack.[1]

A study by the Co-op and the British Red Cross[2] has revealed that over 9 million people in the UK across all adult ages are either often or always lonely, while another study, carried out for the Jo Cox Commission,[3] claims that three quarters of old people regularly report feelings of isolation. An estimated 8 million men, meanwhile, have admitted to similar sensations that all too frequently rise like a bruise; for nearly 3 million of them, it's a daily occurrence. Research by Sense, the disability charity, shows that up to 50 per cent of disabled people will be lonely on any given day.[4] Sundays are particularly guilty of exacerbating loneliness in anyone prone to it, and the Christmas period can be an open wound.

Refugees and migrants face a great many issues, of course, among them housing, discrimination and lingering poverty; those who do manage to settle successfully report that a nagging sense of isolation limits any potential for assimilating into their new environment. Not that all settled refugees particularly like the concept of assimilation itself, as we shall see later.

So its presence in modern society is palpable, the most common of ailments. And yet, despite its clear prevalence and in some cases unavoidable ubiquity, it remains a tricksy subject. It is something that is hard to admit to, to others as much as to oneself, not even in a climate where we are increasingly facing up to our personal issues, anxiety and depression among them. Many might consider loneliness a confession too far, a sign of too much vulnerability, a shameful failing. But this is something we must challenge. The human condition is not a failing. And we need to recognise, too, that we are more and more being encouraged to be, and remain, isolated creatures living in our own individual bubbles. Society, which evolves at the same queasy pace as the technology that powers it, is suffering in ways perhaps we never quite saw coming. As we move away from family and friends into ever-swelling cities in pursuit of work and careers – more of us than ever are now living alone – so we become increasingly focused on our phones to help keep us connected. But 'connection' no longer quite means what it used to, and being repeatedly swiped left in pursuit of love rarely serves as a good boost for morale. Friends on Facebook are not necessarily friends in real life. One's Twitter followers are unlikely to make ideal wedding guests.

And so in today's workplace, we toil away in our little capsules alongside other people whom we barely register. When the situation arises where we actually need to communicate directly with them, we are far more likely to type out a message than lean over and actually speak. Many people now work from home these days, or else in so-called third spaces. Those who do choose to take their laptops somewhere public – a café, the library, or the open-plan reception areas of certain hip hotels that rely on the presence of beards and tortoiseshell spectacles to help boost their TripAdvisor rating — do so with an almost monomaniacal attitude, staring only, and exclusively, at their screens. Why talk to the person next to you and risk an upturned nose for your efforts when you can message an old friend you've not seen for years online?

But then we've come to love our screens, to rely whole-heartedly on them. They are so faithful to us, so loyal. We gaze at them, protect them, and consult with them far more than we do our parents, friends or children. They are our portal to the rest of the world, and the rest of the world is always far more interesting than whatever may be happening around us — even if, strictly speaking, it actually isn't. Our screens obsess us nonetheless. Why else do we walk into lampposts, tumble up and down escalators, or lose threads in verbal conversations that in many cases we ourselves have initiated? Whether it's social media, sports or news outlets, online porn, or whatever else our screens may offer up, they command more of our time than all the flesh and blood around us.

Conversation has fallen silent. We've learned to talk with our thumbs more than our voices. Friends have been relegated to avatars, emojis, and we have reduced ourselves, correspondingly, to two-dimensionalised beings, idealising ourselves through a series of selfies that offer categorical 'proof', exclusively of the inverted comma'd kind, that our lives are perfect, and that we are perfect, too. See my six-pack as I recline on this lounger on the beach! Look at me surrounded by my friends! My smile is sincere, honest!

The communication we indulge in has been largely stripped of its subtlety, its grammar and, perhaps inevitably, any semblance of genuine feeling, if only because genuine feeling requires rather more than 140 characters to fully express itself. So we 'like' rather than verbally empathise; we tweet a turd instead of calling up that friend to commiserate. A 2017 YouGov poll suggested that the 18–34 demographic no longer likes talking to people. We have all fallen out of the habit for the simple reason that it is now possible to do so. While the older generation still actively engage in the assumed pointlessness of small talk, millennials have done away with it altogether. We order online; we opt for the self-checkouts in the supermarket, and bag our own groceries. The rise of Uber might mean we still have to suffer chit-chat with SatNav-reliant taxi drivers, but driverless cars should do away with that tiresome requirement altogether soon enough.

The very concept of interaction as we know it, knew it, then, has become diluted. Technology has made our lives simpler as it has robbed us of what it is that makes us, made us, human.

This is both progress and problematical, and the problem is progressively global. In 2013, The New York Times reported that one in three Americans over the age of 45 identifies as 'chronically lonely', the most severely affected among them partly responsible for driving up the suicide statistics year-on-year.[5]

In Japan, over half a million teenagers and young adults are increasingly living in an exclusively virtual world – attending school virtually, interacting with friends online, and living almost entirely on their Samsungs – and have been labelled accordingly as a measurable demographic, the 'hikikomori', a term the Japanese Health, Labour and Welfare Ministry uses to define those who haven't left their homes or interacted with others for at least six months.

Open a newspaper, any newspaper (or browse it, for free, online), and it can seem like new research is being carried out all the time, much of it reported, and discussed, and commented upon. In early 2018, a new study by Cancer Research UK found that young adults were around 20 times more likely to never speak to their neighbours than the older generation, while 27 per cent said they had never spoken to a stranger on a bus.[6] In all such studies, the older generation fares better, if 'better' is the correct term here. While 21 per cent of 18- to 24-year-olds reported that they never communicated with the people living next door, 99 per cent of the 55+ age bracket confirmed that they did.

'This research shows an increasing generational divide between how millennials and baby boomers prefer to communicate,' the research concluded, before reasserting the associated health issues of such deliberate isolationist behaviour patterns.

In cities like Vancouver, Canada, the condition of loneliness is now so widespread that it has prompted the mayoral initiative Engaged City, which encourages a greater sense of connectedness among neighbours in an attempt to reverse the crippling sensations of solitude they experience daily. (It's a fascinating, and potentially highly influential, initiative. We'll come back to it.)

The way in which we perceive the world has drastically changed, and we are struggling to adapt. Of course we are.

Adaptation takes time, and so for the time being we continue to indulge in the bad habits that, doctors are increasingly telling us, make us unhealthy and unhappy. When you wake up in the morning, are you more likely to turn to your phone or to your partner? What have you missed? What do you think you have missed? We are hamstrung by a concurrent epidemic, FOMO, the perpetual fear of missing out. Our phones know this only too well, and feed into this new need, working hard against finite battery life to ensure that, wherever possible, we miss out on nothing, not the latest reality TV update, not another royal wedding announcement, not even the most recent Kardashian calamity. Or Brexit; we need to keep abreast on Brexit. Trump, too. North Korea. And the impending third, and final, world war. Without Wi-Fi, we'd be lost.

But in the midst of all this, we are becoming more and more like strangers to one another, as more and more we lose the skill to interact with those around us. And so it is inevitable that we are all feeling increasingly alone, looking over our collective shoulders and wondering whether everyone else is starting to feel like us, too.

How else to say it? It's the modern malaise, a new world we have – perhaps unwittingly – created for ourselves.

I am writing these words in my garden office. The door to it is firmly closed, lest I encourage the attentions of my neighbour, one of whom is near-nakedly sunbathing, the other hanging washing on the line. After my wife and children have gone to work and school respectively, and until they come back again, I will see no one at all. The vast majority of my day's interactions will take place online, via email. If I'm lucky, I'll get a text message. If it's a blue moon, a phone call from a friend. The only other time the phone rings, it's from worker bees in call centres whose concern over mis-sold PPI is a salaried necessity.

Face-to-face interaction is almost unheard of. The postman, perhaps, when he knocks, and he doesn't always, or else intermittent visits from Amazon, Jehovah's Witnesses, and that heavyset man with the Geordie accent asking if I want any fresh fish this week.

In relation to my antecedents, my life is almost preposterously isolated. Maximum security prisoners get more one-to-one contact than I do. So, perhaps more by modern-day circumstance than sociopathic choice, I find myself living a life of pronounced solitude. But am I lonely? Would I benefit, both psychologically and physiologically, from communicating more directly with my fellow human beings, people with whom I might share a common outlook or purpose, with whom I might have a laugh, and in whose very presence I might be reminded, because I often need it, that I'm not in fact increasingly all alone in this world?

Wouldn't we all?

Before her senseless murder in the summer of 2016, the MP for Batley and Spen, Jo Cox, set up the Commission on Loneliness, with an aim to address the full impact the condition has on so many different people in society, and to focus on the positive action we can take to recognise it, to build up connections with other people, and help ourselves help everybody else.

Jo had identified that social isolation was an increasing problem, that there was a crisis of fragmentation within our multicultural society that enabled the condition, and effectively promulgated it. At a governmental level, she found that no one was really doing anything much about it, and so she decided to do something herself. She worked assiduously on setting up an agenda, and was due to launch the Loneliness Commission when a single, inexplicable action on 16 June, 2016, meant that she would never be able to see her plans through to fruition.

That day, a Thursday, was an ordinary day for the 41-year-old MP. She had just attended a constituency meeting when she was attacked by a 52-year-old man, Tommy Mair, who shot her and stabbed her multiple times while shouting repeatedly, 'Britain first.' He was later jailed for life.

The fallout from Jo Cox's death was widespread, a communal sense of dizzying bewilderment that a woman with so much to live for, and so little reason for being targeted in such a way, was killed. The collective shock produced ripples you could reach out and touch. Barack Obama, then President of the United States, reached out to the family to offer his condolences, giving this national story an international reach. Then, as so often seems to happen after a tragedy, natural and otherwise, people felt moved to act – in this case, to help build Jo's legacy. In the weeks and months that followed, public goodwill rapidly snowballed, and 50,000 people signed up to a crowdfunding site that pledged a total of £2 million in her memory to ensure that what she had started with the Loneliness Commission would not simply be snuffed out. Her efforts, and her name, would live on.

And they have. The Commission became a cross-party initiative co-chaired by the Labour MP Rachel Reeves and the Conservative

MP Seema Kennedy. Working in close conjunction with partners like Action for Children, Age UK, the Alzheimer's Society, the Campaign to End Loneliness and the Eden Project Communities, they worked towards making loneliness a treatable condition by encouraging us all to look out for one another more, to get back a sense of closely linked neighbourhoods, and to build them up where previously there were none, and to make that connection to others as we would hope others might make with us in times of need. Generally, to be kind to all, simply because it is within all our emotional scopes to do so.

Why *wouldn't* we be kind to others?

The premise of this book – to address loneliness, to chart how it manifests itself, and to highlight initiatives that might help overcome it, perhaps even remove it entirely from our lives – might sound like a tall order. And it is. Aiming to eradicate the problem of social isolation in what can seem like a time riven by so much division and discord is, admittedly, little more than a fanciful utopian ideal. But let's not be too concerned with utopian ideals here, and instead focus on highlighting achievable goals in an environment that isn't, in point of fact, overwhelmingly negative. These are not the dark days certain media outlets might wish us to believe they are. The world is not an increasingly unfriendly, alien place. There are some amazing people out there, running many inspirational initiatives that offer help, succour, a place of warmth, and that proof of kindness. They are out there. You just need to know where to look.

And so this book is an extension of what Jo Cox started, a continuation of the conversation. It will address the growing problems around loneliness in a world increasingly, if unwittingly, designed to foster it, and we will tell the stories of those afflicted, how it descends, and how it affects different people for different reasons. This is not by any measure a traditional self-help book. There will be few bullet points, little bold print, scant exclamation marks – though at the end of most chapters, there will be a directory of organisations that are on hand to help.

But it is a book full of help and guidance nevertheless, and its ultimate aim is to get us all to recognise loneliness in all its guises. What's it like to be crippled by such a social stigma, and why is it a stigma in the first place? What are the ways around it? We will meet those who have suffered from it, and those who still do, and we will examine what they are doing to help themselves, to whom they turned and, in doing so, highlight the work of the people who are helping them.

And there really are those people out there ready and willing to help, friendly armies, empathetic collectives. Because in hearing these stories of loneliness, and in discovering whom it affects and why, we come to realise that it affects everyone, all of us, at some point in our lives, in some way. The tacit suggestion that runs through these pages, then, is that we should all reach out and connect more, and that there are so many ways of doing so, across all sectors of society, people like you, people like me.

As we so often see in the wake of calamitous international events, communities can and frequently do come together all the time. They build bridges, they reach out. They care. Empathy endures. Jo Cox envisaged nothing less than a better world, but it is pertinent to remember that Jo was always more pragmatist than idealist. Had she lived, she would have put that pragmatism into action. Today, others are doing it in her name.

And so, though loneliness can sometimes seem like an insurmountable problem, something impossible to overcome, in fact it isn't.

It really isn't.

ONE

The silent scourge

If it isn't easy pinpointing a condition as nebulous as loneliness, try getting the general public to accept it as a subject worth paying attention to. Loneliness isn't new. It's been around for as long as we have. It might be as damaging to the soul as bread is to the gluten-intolerant, but you can't see loneliness, you can't spread jam on it. It is too intangible.

Early on in our history as a species, we not only survived but prospered by gathering together. We instinctively understood the benefits of collective effort. It was the gathering together of us all that provided mutual protection and assistance. Being alone was something to be avoided. And so while the sensation of loneliness is an unpleasant one, historically speaking it was also a dangerous one. As a result, our brains have evolved to emphasise self-preservation whenever we find ourselves on the social perimeter. The more time we spend on the edges of society, the more we come to fear and mistrust it, our thought process now thoroughly tainted. It is this slow drip of negativity that ultimately permeates our entire physiology and makes us, in the long term, unhealthy.

This is a comparatively new discovery, and it's a fascinating one. It is getting a lot of traction in the medical world, but in the rest of the world, where everything has to clamour for headlines if we are to pay attention, loneliness clearly needed one of its own. Now, thanks to recent studies into the full extent of its negative effects, it has one: *Loneliness kills*.

'Oh, no doubt about it, it's a toxic way to live,' says Steve Cole.

Steve Cole is a genomic researcher at the University of Los Angeles, and a professor of medicine. His work involves looking at how psychological, social and economic conditions can turn into disease and death. Over the past decade, he says, studies into loneliness have concluded something rather unambiguous: that it is among the most dangerous conditions we could possibly encounter in life.

And that, let me tell you, was a surprise, because like all of us, I thought it was more of an annoying nuisance than anything else. Didn't you? But, no. It's worse. We think a lot of things in life are bad – benzene in the water, being heavily overweight, smoking like a chimney – and so in comparison you might think that loneliness is relatively minor. But it's actually a highly toxic way to live, and the epidemiology on this couldn't be clearer: pound for pound, it ranks right up there with the very worst of the biochemical risk factors.

In 2008, the American scientist and writer John Cacioppo, who now lectures at the University of Chicago, wrote a ground-breaking book on the subject, *Loneliness: Human Nature and the Need for Social Connection*.[7] Cacioppo's findings, drawn from research on brain imaging, analysis of blood pressure, the immune response, stress hormones, behaviour patterns and gene expressions, revealed just how interdependent human beings are. In other words, *we need each other*. From the aforementioned historical perspective, solitude has been anathema to us, something humans have worked hard to avoid. We have opted to live in societies for good reason. Within a society, we have everything to gain and, correspondingly, everything to lose. Everything pivots on how well or how poorly we manage our need for human connection. The worse we become in maintaining those connections, the more precarious our health becomes.

There were studies done on mice to see how they dealt with the issue of threat. They inserted into a cage of small mice a bigger, more aggressive one. This bigger, more aggressive one promptly lived up to stereotype by bullying his new cage-mates accordingly. The biology of the smaller mice was then studied, and found a very clear set of threat responses in the body.

Cacioppo then extended his research in a decade-long study in Chicago, this time with humans, a collection of people that identified as chronically lonely, alongside those who believe themselves to be functioning, socially networked people. Steve Cole talks me through the results.

'It floored us by how unambiguous they were,' he says. 'In almost every case, those that had identified as lonely now had the same biology as those bullied mice: in perpetual fight or flight mode.'

Their sense of loneliness was directly affecting their white blood cells, and so they were becoming more prone to incidents like heart attacks and cancer far more quickly than the non-lonely people were. This was the proof that they had long pursued, then: loneliness inadvertently contributes to ill health, because these had all otherwise been healthy individuals. When they became sick, loneliness was to blame.

'And so, no, it might not kill us immediately, but it will nevertheless hasten our demise,' Steve Cole says.

In 2017, these findings created much hubbub within the press. The *Loneliness Kills* headlines were repeated often, alongside: 'THE SILENT EPIDEMIC!' As scaremongering goes, this was effective stuff. But it was also perhaps too excitable, too desperate to claim its exclamation mark.

The author Sara Maitland, who has written with great persuasive elegance on the many benefits of solitude – in 2014, she wrote the illuminating book *How to Be Alone* – tells me that, 'if loneliness is an epidemic, then it has to be "infectious". Otherwise, we are guilty of hyperbolic panic stirring.' She has a point. The loneliness 'virus' is cultural, not bacterial. It's not *that* kind of disease.

It seems to me that we have done a great deal of work on identifying the virus and suggesting treatments for it, but very little on prevention or safe practice. For many infectious diseases, vaccination and inoculation have proved global game-changers. How this works is by giving people harmless low doses of the source of the infection before they come into contact with the illness. But we are so over-socialising our children that, with regard to loneliness, they get no immunity.

Psychologists can argue as long as they like that the human species is naturally designed to be communal and social, Maitland continues,

> ...but anyone who has brought up a child knows that the basic rules of community – share your toys; don't bite; games are more fun if no one cheats; say thank you to your granny; think about other people's feelings – do not come naturally to a two-year-old. We *teach* them, and we do so by instruction, by example, by offering them positive experiences. So I really do believe that the experience of loneliness is growing exponentially because children are not learning its positives, or how they can balance these against the often cruel exclusions of the social group and, elsewhere, the inevitable losses of life – like partner breakups, bereavements, etc. How do we raise young people with self-esteem if we deprive them of opportunities to spend positive time with themselves? Because being by yourself doesn't necessarily mean you have to be lonely, does it?

It is pertinent, of course, to point out that we seem rather to have lost the ability to be alone. As long as we are online, we are never truly alone as we once were, and so the moment we are, we don't quite know what to do. We are more obsessed over battery life than we ever have been at any point in history. It's our batteries that keep us connected. And so inevitably younger generations will struggle even more than older ones when their phones die and they find themselves alone, thoroughly disconnected. What on earth will they do? How will they cope? They are not, in the most fundamental sense, prepared for this.

Elsewhere, several commentators also took umbrage against the Jo Cox Commission's 2017 report[8] that loneliness was now as deadly as smoking. 'This is basically my position,' tweeted one science writer in swift response to the screeching headlines. 'Smoking: definitely very bad for you, repeatedly shown in good epidemiological trials. Loneliness: probably bad for you in some sense but there are lots of tricksy things to tease out of the data.'

Fair enough, of course, but one overriding fact nevertheless remains: loneliness is a miserable state, and it affects more people than ever before. In some cases it destroys lives. This is the situation we have undeniably found ourselves in, irrespective of the factors that got us here. Consequently, we would all do something about it, if we had the knowledge, the skill set.

What this book aims to illustrate is that many of us, even in the depths of our own very private loneliness, possess just that.

Given our historical propensity for gathering together, then, life in the modern world brings threats we never fully saw coming. A great many of us have lost the ability to relax; if we are not working all the time, we are nevertheless 'on', our brains tireless but also frazzled, and constantly in need of another hit of dopamine, to which we have all become accustomed, and addicted. As Steve Cole says,

We are all exhausted, all hustling all of the time, scurrying around in our social rat races, trying to get by in this technologically driven world. And so when we feel stressed by life, or threatened by the people around us, we are turning on – completely without knowing it – those biological defence reflexes that have been baked into our evolved wiring for many years, for eons. They are getting us ready, these programs, to be wounded. Once upon a time, when we felt threatened, we were running from a sabre-tooth tiger. There are no sabre-tooth tigers any more, but we are still running those systems now. Every time we feel socially threatened and socially insecure, these biological defences come on.

One reason for this, according to Cole, might be the role of social media in our lives, how it doesn't allow us to switch off in the way we once would. It is a cliché to suggest that we live in a fast and demanding world, but the fact is we do. Emails are sent to be responded to swiftly, Facebook posts to be liked. We don't have to check in with a friend's – or, just as commonly, a nemesis's – Instagram feed, but we do so because we can't help it. Social media has been designed to be continually refreshed and replenished and updated, and so we are struggling to adapt accordingly. We have become needy. We never switch off. FOMO.

'Social media has a propensity for amplifying the very worst of human tendencies,' Cole says. 'Partly because it's entertaining. It is fascinating to us when we see awkward, private moments of others going viral, when we read online trolling, and when we read about the victims of those trollings. Sad as that may be, it is nevertheless true.'

He cites, as an example, perhaps the inevitable one: Facebook. 'Facebook works to understand you as a social being, and then exploits you for marketing purposes. There is just this endless predation on what initially was supposed to be one of the core sources of succour and safety in a person's life.'

For Steve Cole, this is personal. Years previously, he had worked in Silicon Valley, where he says he spent much of his time trying hard to bend technology towards ultimate good. 'But I failed. The forces of marketing are so much stronger than that, and so right now, it still seems to bring out the worst in us.'

But this strand of technology is still in its relative infancy. It is new to us, and so remains an exciting novelty. The revolution ushered in by our phones has brought with it a new language, alongside new ways of behaving and interacting with others. We are still learning its parameters, and how we are supposed to behave when we are on social media. We overstep these parameters frequently, and some of us seem to go out of our way to abuse it, convinced that the thrill it gives us is a good thing. But, argues Steve Cole, we will learn from these mistakes in time. The more victims there are, the greater the fallout, and the more we will ultimately have to rethink these ways of communication. Self-moderation will come, he suggests, but only in time.

Right now, social media is still a high school popularity contest where everybody criticises everybody else, or else allows us to heap adulation upon ourselves and our immediate circle by posting idealised versions of our highly edited lives for others to admire, to compliment and envy. We need to get back to a more mature and compassionate, and ultimately pro-social, human-oriented sense of our lives, as sappy as that sounds, and to put technology in its place. Continue the useful aspects of it, certainly, but also learn to get rid of the sick, obsessional versions that seem simply to prey on our insecurities.

He insists that he is confident this will come to pass, that the emerging generation will at some point grow bored of our current obsession with social media, and will want to move on to other things.

Kids are basically programmed to tire of whatever they were doing today, and do something else tomorrow. But we, the adults, have had this technology seep into us, so we are not quite so well defended as they are. Nevertheless, I am cautiously optimistic that as young people grow up as digital natives, they will eventually realise that: hey, this stuff makes me feel bad.

At which point, I ask, they'll stop it, and learn how to police themselves? Steve Cole smiles. 'Hopefully,' he says.

According to John Cacioppo's research, there are two general kinds of loneliness. The first is transient, the kind we are all prone to feel from time to time, when, for example, we move to a new city or go off to college, or in some other way endure a major social disruption to the fabric of our lives. But this kind is largely fleeting. We mostly succeed in establishing new relationships, and so that initial sense of painful deprivation ultimately recedes.

'In these cases, the biology isn't yet instantaneously toxic, it isn't chronic,' says Steve Cole. 'So transient situational loneliness doesn't have huge long-term consequences on us, though of course it does have short-term biological impacts.'

It is the other kind that is more insidious, more harmful. The effects of chronic loneliness are more far-reaching. And that's because, says Cole, 'it becomes a lifestyle. When you

21

have loneliness as a lifestyle, then there are huge health risks. The diseases they engender may take decades to build up, but they build up nevertheless. So if you have a heart attack today because of it, that hasn't happened overnight. It's been brewing for at least a decade.'

Invariably, it is chronic loneliness that proves the harder to treat. By the time loneliness has developed into something severe, the sufferer tends to view the world differently. Our social philosophy has become separate from those of our peers, and in some cases we will have stopped believing that people are generally good and decent. Indeed, we will predict that people will very likely disappoint us, simply because we believe it to be so.

A healthy mindset tends to view the world, and its people, as ultimately decent and fair. But those with chronic loneliness have come to believe that the world is pointedly Darwinian, that people will always take advantage of us, and that there really is no shelter from the storm and chaos of the human experience. As our perception of the social world gets worse, our biology starts to foster these diseases that lurk complacently within us until the point at which they are complacent no longer.

Our challenge, then, is a considerable one: to help those with transient loneliness by encouraging them to reconnect to the community around them; and also to attempt to eradicate the more ruminative conditions that feed into loneliness when it starts to tip towards the chronic.

Loneliness and depression are often confused, though the two conditions are distinct, separate things. As John Cacioppo writes in his book, feeling socially isolated means that one wants to be close to others but feels uncertain about whom one can confide in, depend or trust. And so loneliness refers to *how people feel about their social connections*. Depression, on the other hand, refers to how people feel in general. Because one can lead into the other, a person may feel both lonely and depressed. However, one can only be depressed for reasons other than loneliness, and loneliness does not always lead to depression.

While every one of us is susceptible to both states, at least 50 per cent of us will be more predisposed to loneliness because we have inherited it. We are all susceptible to situational factors, but what is heritable, Cacioppo writes, is, 'the intensity of pain felt when one feels socially isolated.' In other words, some of us will be able to put up with being alone more than others; some may even come to value their isolation. But because it diminishes the brain's executive functioning, it is more difficult for people who feel lonely to control their impulses. It's a slippery slope that slides, often directly, towards increasingly poor health. As a result of it, we might stop exercising, because what's the point? We cease in our pursuit for a healthy diet, and turn instead to comfort food, junk food. The more unhappy we feel, the more unsafe, too. Successive dominoes start to topple.

And so what do the experts suggest we do? In his book, Cacioppo posits no pat answers but does at least offer up something, a mnemonic – EASE – for those who might be looking for easy answers. EASE stands for Extend Yourself, Action Plan, Selection and Expect the Best. Each requires effort, but the effort, he assures, will be worth it. He encourages us to break out of our confines and reintroduce ourselves to the neighbourhood, the wider community. Volunteer at local shelters, the nearest hospital, charity shops. Teach older people to use computers, or tutor children. Read to the blind. Stop being passive. Be active, effective. The more positive our outlook, the more in control we will be over our thoughts and behavioural patterns. In this way, change might come.

The good news is that there are plenty of initiatives out there to help in this way, a selection of which we will look at over the coming chapters. No one, least of all Cacioppo himself, is suggesting that getting rid of loneliness is an easy task, and if you consult with Steve Cole on the matter, he sounds a note of ambivalence about how we are currently dealing with the issue. But he does applaud the effort.

I don't want to sound pessimistic here, but I think a lot of the models of intervention right now are probably going to miss the mark, and here's why: transient loneliness is easier to deal with because, simply, if you gave me more friends, that would fix the problem. But remember that those dealing with chronic loneliness are people who have already developed a belief – and probably a justifiable one, to some extent – that the world is a threatening and unpredictable place. If you take someone with that worldview and then put them together with a bunch of people who feel similarly, then what do you think is going to happen? Are they going to feel better, more supported? No. They would agree that the world sucks, and that you can't trust anybody.

And so this is our defining challenge: to halt the loneliness before it becomes chronic, and to at least try to wrest those with chronic loneliness away from its maw. The effort will be worthwhile. If there still needs to be more sophisticated interventions in dealing with the condition, then there also needs to be a starting point, and this is where we are right now: the starting point. The intention is there.

'You guys, in Europe and across Asia, are definitely making progress, and much better progress than we are here in America,' Steve Cole says, explaining that the American perspective remains a little different from the rest of the world.

Americans still think of themselves as rugged individuals. Our mindset is that we still have to herd our cows on the ranch, and American ideology around trusting and depending upon people – well, if you look at the US historically, you'll see that that's not how we came to be. Thing is, that life doesn't exist any more; we are no longer cowboys. Which is why I admire what you guys are doing in the rest of the world. You are making loneliness part of the big-picture media, and awareness is definitely the first step. Because, from awareness, we can all begin to take the second step, and we can do so creatively.

This is precisely what an increasing number of individuals are now doing in and around the subject: they are being creative, they are finding solutions. The solutions are working. If loneliness has for so long been a stigma, the silent sufferance, then perhaps there is change, real change, for this is a condition people are now actively fighting against.

And a great many of them, as we shall see, are stealthily, steadily, succeeding.

Directory

The Jo Cox Foundation

https://www.jocoxfoundation.org/

Eden Project Communities

https://www.edenprojectcommunities.com/

Two

How to become compassionate

A few months after Dawn Cahill had survived the ruptured aneurysm that had so convincingly threatened to kill her, she felt she needed a change of pace, a new life with a slower momentum to it. A self-confessed urbanite, London had abruptly begun to feel too loud for her after her haemorrhage, too bright and too much, a place of crowds and potholes and rush hours, the endless debris from late-night takeaways, and morning-after mood swings. And so, gradually, in increments, she left the city and headed east, towards a quiet, if not quite remote, part of East Anglia, an hour outside of Norwich. Here she spent the occasional week, then two, then frequent weekends before realising she liked it, a lot. And so she began looking to spend more time there, to perhaps making her stay a permanent one. She now lives in a sedate village, the kind where few wait for the bus because everyone is aware of its erratic timetable. She would never have imagined herself, in her mid-40s, relocating to somewhere so self-consciously quiet and rural, but life has a habit of throwing curveballs.

Brushes with near-death tend to bring out the clichés in those who survive them, and so like many people with similar experiences, Dawn became a changed person. The threat of mortality had brought her up short, and she came to view everything she knew as wrong. Work, she belatedly realised, had been an enormous pressure on her, so she stopped. She shed certain friendships, and allowed the more humdrum ones to drift. Her marriage continued but changed shape, her husband still working in the city during the week, and still living in what had once been the marital home, but commuting on Friday afternoons, after lunch, for long weekends in their new coastal home. Dawn got custody of the dog, a puppy barely a few weeks old when her haemorrhage struck, and here the dog thrived. Things might have been much more complicated had they had children, but their decision to remain childless now seemed, in the light of recent events, a good idea.

Day-to-day life a good hour outside Norwich where the buses seldom ran had an elastic, elliptical feel to it. The clock might still have told the right time twice a day, but clocks were rarely glanced at any more. Lie-ins, once guilty weekend pleasures, had become the norm, while lunch and dinner happened when they happened. Her once typically hectic adult life had mellowed into something more meditative by its very nature, thus allowing her brain to go about its mysterious business of healing itself. Her stress levels began to plateau, and this surprised her. Had she ever fantasised what life might be like after a grave illness, she likely wouldn't have banked on being quite so capable of scaling it down as much as she subsequently felt it necessary to do. Solitude, it transpired, suited her.

'I would walk my dog through the marshes, and along these wide-open beaches, and found that I loved it,' Dawn says. 'I just felt to myself: yes, I might be okay here.'

Her village and its inhabitants moved at her speed, too: a deliberately slow pace, a mile-per-hour average commensurate to the neighbourhood's average age of 60. Dawn, at 45, found herself one of the enclave's younger residents, a virtual hipster in an environment dominated by people long past the national age of retirement. To occupy her days, she began taking wildlife photographs, and posting them on social media sites. She started painting, something she had never done before. She was good, possessed of a natural talent. *Who'd have thought it?*, she privately wondered. The paintings went on to be exhibited locally, in galleries and exhibitions. To her continuing surprise, people liked her abstract watercolours; they sold internationally.

To her new social circle, Dawn was fresh blood, someone to talk to, perhaps even confide in. While she found herself quietly revelling in this new solitude, others saw her presence as a way to help alleviate theirs.

Elsie lived just around the corner. Like Dawn, she had a young dog to help give shape to her days. They would bump into each other regularly most mornings, walking the same nature walks, falling in step with one another while their pets ran ahead.

'She was very friendly, very sweet,' Dawn says of this new friend of hers, four full decades her senior. Elsie had never married and, like Dawn, had had no children. 'She had come close to getting married once, she told me, but her fiancé turned out to be what she called a *wrong 'un*. She said no more about him, and I didn't want to pry.'

Theirs became an acquaintance of convenience, someone to walk the dog with. They only exchanged telephone numbers a few weeks later, when Elsie's dog died suddenly. 'Losing a dog when you are otherwise alone,' says Dawn. 'I knew it just must be one of the very worst things.'

For Elsie, then 83, it was. It takes the death of the only constant companion in your life to make you realise just how alone in the world you really are. Dawn knew that she, Elsie, was grieving, and that she was distraught. 'I felt awful for her.'

Over the next few days and weeks, Elsie's distress manifested itself into a full-blown anxiety. Where previously she might call Dawn once a day for a quick chat, she now called her all the time. When she wasn't speaking to Dawn, she was speaking to other friends, the telephone her only lifeline. The conversations became cyclical in nature, Elsie desperate that her dog had died without warning, so very young, and that she really wanted another one but realised that, at her advanced age, this wouldn't be fair on either her or the new dog. Oh, but the pain. She missed him so terribly, and became increasingly convinced that the only way to get through such a piercing bereavement was to get a replacement. Which she would get, tomorrow – *no*, today.

She would go to the nearest animal sanctuary and... But here she would remember, as if abruptly pulling focus on reality. She was old; her back had been giving her mobility problems. And there was the cat to consider. The cat had predated her old dog, and had suffered him accordingly; it was unlikely that the cat would suffer its replacement quite so willingly.

'I felt so bad listening to her, but as her anxiety got worse, I just felt increasingly incapable of being able to help.' Because Dawn was still coping with her own emotional fallout after her haemorrhage, she buckled. All sorts of stimuli would overwhelm her; she needed rest, and a lot of sleep. But the phone would ring at all hours, Elsie again, and Dawn would have to let it ring out. 'I couldn't cope.'

The guilt at having screened the call would gnaw at her. She couldn't get Elsie out of her head. Elsie then developed high blood pressure and, with it, heart palpitations. One night, late, after bed, she rang Dawn, and this time Dawn answered. Elsie had just put a call into the non-emergency telephone line, 111, reluctant to trouble the actual emergency line, 999, she explained, even though she had been convinced she might be dying. Dawn dressed, and rushed straight over to her house. She was still there when the ambulance arrived.

The paramedics diagnosed panic attack rather than heart attack, and Elsie spent the next few minutes apologising to everyone, and offering them tea.

She told me that she was so sorry to have bothered me, that I had enough on my plate already, and that she didn't want to make things worse. She said she was being silly, overreacting. *What am I like?*, she kept saying. But the fact is, she wasn't being silly at all. The dog *was* her lifeline. She would talk to it; it would keep her company. And now she was all alone.

The stress Dawn had so successfully shed these past few months began to pile back on.

She was lovely, Elsie, and I really did care about her. She was kind, and funny, and I knew that she really didn't want to be a burden on anyone. But I also knew that sometimes you have to set boundaries, especially with new friends, and with me being in the state I was in, I just felt not only that she needed proper help, but that I needed help in helping her.

So Dawn started to research online, seeking ways in which to better assist Elsie with her ongoing anxiety. They continued to speak on the phone every day, and during these conversations, with much delicacy, Dawn suggested that she refer herself to a professional. She told Elsie about organisations she had seen online, like Age UK and The Silver Line (TSL). Christmas was looming, and she knew that Elsie was dreading that time of enforced seasonal cheer.

'She used to buy presents for her dog, and open them on Christmas Day. I'd already invited her over for Christmas morning so that we could open presents for my dog together, but I knew it would ultimately just make her situation all the more painful to bear.'

Elsie listened to Dawn, and took her advice. She called The Silver Line, where operatives listened to her story, and were able to help. Slowly, her anxiety calmed, and she began to deal better with her bereavement. She still calls Dawn once a day, but now Dawn actively looks forward to speaking to her.

> I realised that it doesn't take much out of my day, and more than that, that I enjoy talking to her. I value our conversations. She's really funny, she makes me laugh, and we connect. If I go away for a few days, she tells me that she misses me, that I make her smile, that I cheer her up. She likes having me near, and that's lovely to hear. I suppose I put myself in her position, being as lonely as she was, and in need of nothing more than a friendly voice at the end of a phone line. And so that's what I offer her. I get as much out of our phone calls as she does. She has become a true friend to me, and I value our friendship.

Dawn's instinct to pass Elsie into the hands of the professionals was wise. There are ways and ways to be compassionate, to help those in need, and not all of us know how to do this instinctively. Many need guidance.

It is an average Sunday afternoon on an average 31-day month late into the year. It will be dark soon, the day cruelly curtailed by a sun impatient to set. The phone lines at The Silver Line helpline in Blackpool are thrumming with activity, as they always do on Sunday afternoons. A 2016 poll found that almost three quarters of old people in the UK are lonely, and that more than half have never spoken to anyone about how they feel. In older people, loneliness can bring about an increased risk of high blood pressure and dementia, and such sensations seem to expand and swell evermore piercingly on Sunday afternoons, traditionally a family day, that time of the week when spouses and siblings would get together for the necessary but often satisfying rigmarole of a Sunday lunch together. These kinds of occasion might well have invariably descended into bickering – there can be few more combustible elements in the universe than three generations of the same family gathered around plates of meat and veg – but such wilful dysfunction actually reveals just how all families *do* function: by remaining connected.

For those who have become widowed, whose families have splintered across the country and further still, Sundays no longer revolve around a roast, gravy and all the trimmings. In those homes whose kitchens possess a microwave, the preparation of lunch is no longer an event but rather something that can be magicked up in less time than it takes to boil an egg.

This is why Sunday is TSL's busiest day, when on average they field a new call every minute. Very often, says CEO Sophie Andrews, the people who call don't always immediately identify loneliness as their reason for dialling in. It is a subject to be skirted around until sufficient time for a human bond to successfully foster; only then can such intimacy be broached.

'I remember one particularly memorable story that concerns the gentleman who rang up on Christmas Day to ask us how to cook a chicken,' Andrews says. 'Twenty minutes later, he told us that his wife had died, that they had been married for 60 years, and that he missed her. He would never have told us that in the first minute.'

The Silver Line was launched in the UK in November 2013, the brainchild of Esther Rantzen, erstwhile television and newspaper journalist, and also the person who founded Childline back in the 1980s. Two years earlier, she had written a newspaper article about dealing with her own bereavement, and living alone for the first time. As with so many stories that seem to require the oxygen of a public airing by a noted individual before they can fully resonate on a collective basis, Rantzen's piece struck a universal chord. Millions just like her had also been bereaved, and were struggling with the sensations of extreme isolation. What people saw as her bravery in an article that read like a confessional prompted others to simply say, 'Me too.'

The letters she received from people up and down the UK, Rantzen has subsequently said, came from the 'stiff upper lip' generation, those who often found it difficult to give voice to their feelings, let alone recognise them for themselves. These were individuals who might have called the Samaritans for help, but were just as likely not to. 'They wouldn't want to block the line,' Sophie Andrews says. 'They wouldn't want to be seen as a burden.'

The stigma around loneliness was keenly felt by Rantzen's peers, but it was Rantzen's public confession that allowed them to confess. Realising that what all these people needed was a sympathetic ear, she founded TSL a year later, and launched it initially in the north-west of England, then the north-east, and then extended it into the more rural communities of the Isle of Man and Jersey. This was to test its feasibility: would anybody call in? There were already many so-called befriending services up and down the country, but research had suggested that people often didn't know where to turn for help. This, then, might prove a single point of contact. Would the service they were offering be required?

The answers were: yes, and yes. The calls flooded in. Deemed by the Centre for Social Justice as an outstanding success, TSL began a 24-hour free and confidential helpline a year later, employing at first a regular staff of just two, alongside some game volunteers. On its launch day, 3102 calls were registered. The numbers have gone up steadily ever since. The charity now employs 200 personnel, the phone lines manned by both full-time paid staff alongside hundreds of volunteers. The volunteers are often people who had once called in for help themselves.

Multiple studies have shown that older people can slip out of society as they age, all too easily sidelined and forgotten. For these people, then, TSL has become as much a lifeline as helpline. A great many calls come overnight from carers whose partners have dementia and Alzheimer's, or they are perhaps suffering from anxiety and depression. As Andrews points out: 'At two o'clock in the morning, they are not going to call their daughters to say they are feeling all alone, unsupported and lonely, are they?'

They could always call social services, of course, but a call to social services might have ramifications. An elderly person struggling to look after an elderly spouse could prompt intervention when, really, intervention is not yet needed, not least if all that person really wants is to sound off to someone else at the end of a phone line in their moment of need.

'A lot of older people simply don't want to be a burden on their family,' says Andrews, 'and so a lot of people who are 80 and 90 years old, that generation where they just got on with it, simply accept it as their "lot", really have nowhere else to turn.'

For a still comparatively new charity, TSL is in rude health. Between the years 2016 and 2017, it formed a high-profile partnership with Marks & Spencer, and announced the Duchess of Cornwall as their first Royal Patron, to coincide with Camilla's 70th birthday. The helpline now averages around 10,000 calls per week, 90 per cent of which come from first-time callers. The primary reason for calling is loneliness, an indication that many of these people, as many as 80 per cent of them, live alone, with no one else to talk to. The majority of callers are women: 60 per cent, and the average age is 70+.

In addition to its helpline, TSL also directs its efforts into more regular loneliness-abating initiatives, for those who crave more personalised, and more frequent, one-to-one contact. There are telephone and letter-writing friendship services, in which so-called Silver Liners are paired with a hand-picked volunteer, someone with whom they might share common interests. And so, all over the country, on any given day of the week, people are writing letters, and placing phone calls, to those who were once cut off but now no longer are.

'It all works very well,' says Sophie Andrews.

Directory
The Silver Line
https://www.thesilverline.org.uk/
0800 4 70 80 90

Three

Contacting the elderly

Jack King, who lives along England's southern coast, is a 96-year-old recipient of TSL's weekly phone calls. Jack, who had joined the army at 15 as part of the Royal Artillery, and later spent part of the Second World War held captive in a Japanese prison camp, was married for almost 65 years until his wife died in 2010.

Like many of those who use TSL's services, Jack felt reluctant to ask for help. 'I suppose because my generation did everything for themselves,' he tells me. 'But I had a lot of hours on my own, and I had to fill them some way.'

He did at least have ways of keeping busy: he wrote, he painted and played music, but still was keenly aware of his new isolation. Old war injuries were compromising his mobility, and the recent onset of macular degeneration was making several of his favourite pastimes difficult to continue. So today, once a week, on the phone, he talks to a lady called Hannah, a forty-something Londoner he was paired with via TSL.

'She doesn't do creative writing, she doesn't paint and doesn't play music,' Jack points out, 'but she's very chatty, very intelligent and funny, and we talk about, oh, all sorts of things. I've come to depend on my phone calls to her because they make my day.'

The Silver Line's objective here is nothing if not realistic. No one is claiming to be able to give Jack back what he has lost, but TSL never did claim to cure loneliness, or bereavement. But, says Sophie Andrews,

… what we do aim to do is help people improve their self-confidence. If you are lonely and isolated, then talking to someone once a week, or using the helpline whenever you might need it, can get you to a point where you are able to re-engage better with the community around you. So that's what we're aiming to do: to give people that gentle assistance, to get them back on their feet, and assert themselves once more.

Gabriella Herrick is another of their volunteers. If the average volunteer has an average age of 55, then Gabriella is somewhat atypical. Just 30 years old, she is an architect working and living in London, and in many ways is the quintessential young urban adult, juggling a burgeoning career with flatshare commitments and a boyfriend. She loves to travel, and is a big fan of classical music. Spare time is something she squeezes into whatever is left outside working hours. This isn't much, she admits, but then Gabriella is good at making time. Two years ago, amidst the endless demands of her life, she realised that something was missing: the presence of, and connection with, older people. Her own grandparents had died when she was still in her teens, and she found herself increasingly craving the kind of connection that only comes cross-generationally. She also missed the art of letter-writing in a world otherwise dominated by screens.

'So one day I googled *letter-writing services*, and found my way to Age UK, which in turn directed me to The Silver Line,' she explains. Originally from a small town in South Wales, Gabriella had had a fleeting experience of big-city isolation herself when she first arrived in London, but ultimately she believes she was lucky. 'I lived with friends, so I was never fully alone. But being in a place with just so many people around you all the time, people that didn't know one another, made me realise that feeling lonely could be the worst thing in the world, especially if you are older, when friends and family members have dropped off.'

Gabriella seems to be one of those quietly heroic types, instinctively philanthropic, the sort who will always help people whenever possible. If, for example, she sees an elderly person struggling with their shopping, she will go and offer help; if someone is looking lost, she will do her best with directions. When she learned of TSL's letter-writing initiative, she knew that this was an ideal fit.

The vetting process, however, was diligent and rigorous. 'Oh, there was all sorts of protocol and etiquette,' she laughs. 'It's a little like a dating website, to be honest. You have to fill in things like your locality, your interests, what you do for work.

The whole thing took weeks, if not months. Then there is a phone interview to further gauge your suitability, and after that I was sent a training booklet to study.'

But at the end of it, success. She was deemed an ideal candidate, and was matched with Keith, 82, a retired architect.

And I have to say, it's been a lovely experience, a lovely thing to do. I enjoy the process of actually writing to him. Letters give you a time to reflect, and so phone calls, texts and emails – none of these are the same thing at all. I found that I enjoyed taking the time to fully express myself over the course of a long letter, reflecting over what I've done, and also encouraging Keith to write to me about whatever he might want to discuss.

TSL recommends that each letter extends to at least four pages of A4, and that it offers a healthy balance between sharing information (but not too much), and also asking questions that require of the penpal more than a yes/no answer. If the art of letter-writing is largely a lost one, then TSL aims, where possible, to revive it. Participants are encouraged not to get too personal – and every letter is read by a staff member, as part of their safeguarding protocol, before being forwarded on to the Silver Liner – but rather to let the Silver Liner lead, at his or her own pace.

Gabriella only knows of Keith what Keith has been happy to share with her. She tells me that the very act of letter-writing itself encourages the kind of respectful manner that seems otherwise outdated today, even antiquated.

'I find it all rather charming. But I was very hesitant with the first few letters, because really, what should I say? Then I worried whether Keith would be able to read my writing. But we quickly turned out to be a very good match.'

Of her penpal she knows only that he is based somewhere south-west of London, and that he lives alone. He has not mentioned a partner, or children, though he does refer, in his letters, to nieces and nephews.

'But all of that doesn't matter, really, because we find so many other things to talk about, so many common interests: architecture, obviously, but also classical music – he loves it, I play it – and travel. We both love Italy, and so the letters just flow.'

When I ask Gabriella whether she would ever like to meet up with Keith – something TSL does not recommend between its letter-writers – she shrugs and says, yes, sure, 'for a pint, maybe.' But meeting up with your penpal might well change the dynamic, and, argues TSL, they would prefer, wherever possible, to maintain that dynamic. These are relationships designed to flourish in ink, on paper.

'And,' says Gabriella, 'it's perfect like this. I don't have any other relationships in my life like this one, and I suppose that's why it feels like such a special connection.'

Gabriella's Keith is Keith Frow, the man to whom she writes so diligently each month. He lives in an unprepossessing block of flats in Sussex, alone, and is mostly housebound. Like Jack King, he is nothing if not the product of his era: pragmatic, uncomplaining, implacable.

'Oh, I can deal with loneliness, all right,' he tells me in what I quickly come to realise is his typical matter-of-factness. 'I busy myself enough. I read a lot, I listen to music – television not so much – but I've always been able to spend long periods of time by myself. Which is not to say I would necessarily do so if my choices were different, mind you, but they are not, so…'

Keith spent his career in the world of architecture, and in his time belonged to many associated organisations. He was once a Friend of the English National Opera, for example, and had been a member of the British Museum. 'I belonged to lots of groups where I had lots of contacts, lots of friends, people I would meet socially, and with whom I had plenty in common,' he says. 'But one of the many consequences of living to old age is that those people I used to know and socialise with are either dead, or in a similar position to myself these days: housebound.'

Lamenting the loss of daily human contact, he called Age Concern one day a few years back, and was directed to The Silver Line. He is now the recipient of a one-to-one weekly phone call, and, separately, writes to Gabriella at least once every three weeks.

'I do find it's nice to have a little regular communication with someone,' he says.

It plugs a gap, one of many which has opened up in my life. It doesn't plug all of them, of course – I'm still alone – but then it doesn't pretend to. As I see it, loneliness and isolation are facts of life, and there is nothing you can do about facts of life.

You have to face them, because that is what life is all about. No point getting suicidal over it. No. You simply do the best you can. I think people in my position would feel extremely lucky that they had lived so long, so all I am trying to do now is to fill those few gaps in my days, and to spend the rest of my time doing the things I like. I've always loved reading, and listening to music. Now more than ever.

Quite suddenly, he frowns. 'But not rap, by the way. A lot of the new music, I find, makes me feel 300 years old. I know quite a lot of intelligent people who seem to like it, but it just strikes me as one hell of a noise...'

To Gabriella, he writes about architecture, how it was in his day, and how it is in hers – Gabriella's London firm specialises in conservation, so they connect a lot over this – and about music that extends way beyond rap, hip-hop and grime.

Gabriella plays the cello and violin, and she is a very busy woman, clearly. Like many young adults these days, she lives some considerable distance from home. Of course, when I was younger, families tended to live together, the houses were larger, and so you ended up looking after family members as they aged, your aunts and uncles and so on. Whether everyone was happy with that situation or not was always open to question, but you were all together. Today, people don't seem to want to be together quite so much. They want their own houses, flats; their own space. The consequence of that, however, is that they might start to feel cut off and, I suppose, a little isolated.

I sometimes wonder whether, as another consequence, young people have lost the art of conversation. It seems to me that they can't always talk very well, as if they have all these feelings – the product of stress – but struggle to put such thoughts into words.

He pauses here, as if struggling over words himself.

I might be exaggerating all this, of course, and I might have it all wrong, but it seems to me that the way life is lived now is more stressful upon people; it doesn't allow emotions to be properly expressed. Life seems more hectic today: all these computers, all these emails. I'm not in a position to say whether life is better or worse now than it was when I was younger, because I don't know, frankly. Who's to say? But the sense I have is that life does move very quickly. It's one big rush.

And so Keith, housebound and resigned to old age's stricter parameters, watches modern life unfold from his vantage point with gentle bemusement and a certain relief at being one step removed from it. He accepts his own isolation, as he says, as an unavoidable consequence of being 82, but he still takes active pleasure in the arts, in conversation, in his letter-writing. When I ask him what I asked his penpal earlier, whether they might ever like to meet up after two years of such assiduous contact, he deflects the suggestion immediately, reminding me that Gabriella is young and far away, and far too busy. Their relationship is a perfectly formed thing as it is. Why attempt to extend, and perhaps complicate, it?

But still, I wonder whether he is curious about her, even about what she might look like? We live in times where fact-checking – more specifically: snooping, *spying* – is a part of everyday online life. Gabriella herself has a solid social media presence, and so I ask Keith whether he has ever googled her, simply out of idle curiosity?

His response is beautiful, and for the rest of the day I cherish it.

'*Googled?*' he repeats, his voice raising very nearly a full octave, 'what's *googled?*'

Bob Lowe had been married to his wife Kath for 65 years. But, as he is quick to point out, 'we were together, actually, for 70 years. She was 14 when I met her, and I was 16.' The story he tells of their marriage has the ring of fairytale to it: an ideal, and ideally happy, union, three happy children, a rose-tinted, contented life. Relaying it to me, he sounds blissful in recollection. But, eventually, the inevitable happened as their advanced years began to take an increasing toll on Kath's health.

'One day,' Bob says, 'she turned to me and said, *Where is Bob?* And of course that was the most shattering of events, because I am Bob.'

There had, he admits, been prior signs: Kath's increasing forgetfulness, a general sense of slowing down. It took a visit to the doctor to confirm the suspicions Bob himself had been unable to voice: the onset of dementia. The condition evolved with cruel stealth.

'She began to ask me where her mother was. What I wanted to tell her was that her mother had died many years earlier, but that just distressed her, and so I ended up telling her that Mum had gone to the shops; she'll be home soon.'

Bob nursed his wife through five long years of dementia, an endless dark corridor towards an inevitable conclusion. During this time, she fell and broke her leg. The hip replacement that followed went wrong. She became wheelchair-bound. Doctors recommended a care home. But Bob, ever devoted, refused to let her go, to give her up. They had their house in Hampshire modified, and a special medical bed installed. She slowed down, had practically stopped, communication minimal. Bob refused to face it. He nursed his wife day in, day out, as dutiful to her in old age as he had been in youth.

'Things will be better soon,' he'd tell her. 'You'll see.'

And perhaps, in a manner of speaking, he was right. One night in March 2011, Bob's wife of almost seven decades died, her suffering at an end. Her husband was by her side. But the sense of bereavement was felt as an instant devastation.

'She was just… *gone*,' he says now, seven years later. 'Gone.'

His voice catches, and he takes a moment to compose himself. Some people will tell you that bereavement gets easier as the years pass. For Jack King, he grew to find a kind of peace with it. 'It's a dull pain now rather than a sharp pain,' Jack had told me. 'You learn to live with it. You learn.'

For Bob Lowe, it never did get easier. 'People ask me, they say: have I come through the loneliness yet and emerged on the other side? And my answer is always the same: *no*. That's not going to happen. I cannot see it happening. You see, I loved Kath so desperately that it could *never* happen.'

But Bob, ultimately a social soul, was never going to fully hide himself away from the rest of the world. He endeavoured to keep himself busy, and maintained a wide circle of friends. Many friends have, on occasion, asked whether he might ever consider re-marrying. His blue eyes always swell at the very suggestion, the eyebrows creeping above his large-framed glasses.

'*What*, and be unfaithful to her memory?' he says.

It is an overcast day in October when we talk, a 'miserable day', in Bob's words. 'Miserable days are the worst, I find.' His house is filled with photographs documenting the life he has led, and many of them collect upon the mantelpiece in the lounge, 20 to 25 pictures that feature him and Kath throughout their long years together: their wedding, the arrival of their children, and the arrival, years later, of their children's children. They are proof, vivid testament, to a life lived, and to Kath's legacy.

'I've so many memories in this house; they surround me,' he says. 'But I find it's on days like this, when it's miserable outside, and overcast, that the house can seem particularly empty to me. I look all around me, at all the photographs…' His voice catches in his throat again, obstructed by the lump it finds there. 'And they virtually break me down, I'm afraid. Oh gosh, yes.' Rallying, he adds: 'I do love looking at all these photographs, all these memories. But it's not easy.'

He references one particular picture, Kath smiling brightly, her face filling the frame. 'It's as if she is here, with me. And it just breaks me up, I'm afraid.'

A few short years after her death, Bob had a minor accident at home, something that required his doctor's supervision. It was while he was in the surgery that Bob got chatting to the nurse. Bob is good at chatting, and he was already friendly with this particular nurse. He confessed that he was still missing his wife keenly, and she asked him, pointedly, what he was going to do about it? A former development engineer in the plastics industry, Bob didn't really know. He was long retired, and retirement was weighing even more heavily in widowhood. The nurse told him that there were options, many, all sorts of things, and that he might look into them. He had, she told him, a nice speaking voice. Perhaps he could consider lending his crisp consonants and rounded vowels to Talking Newspapers, an online initiative where people read the news for visually impaired listeners.

'And so I did, and I am now a newsreader for the blind,' he states, proudly. Bob being Bob, he has also become the studio director, and has undertaken a lot of its administration. 'I organise the interviews, and I interview people on our little radio station, like our local Lord Mayor, for example. I ask them questions about their lives. It keeps me busy.'

Though he may look his age, or at least close enough to it, Bob doesn't particularly behave the way one might expect a 96-year-old to. He remains robust, fit and healthy, his mind actively sharp. Volunteering, he says, has given him the new lease of life he so clearly needed, and he actively encourages others in his position to do similar. He works as an ambassador for The Silver Line, extolling the palpable virtues of getting out of the house, no matter how hard that might seem. He talks of the importance of re-engaging with the community around you, and the more he himself does this, the more he staves off his own loneliness, or at the very least keeps it partially at bay.

But for Bob, it will only ever be partial. Loneliness, like the monsters of children's nightmares, is forever stalking the perimeter. 'I hate the nights. I have to take sleeping pills now, and that's because I've run into a rather bad patch of dreaming recently. It's very emotionally upsetting.'

What remains so inspiring about Bob, however, is the way he tackles the problem. The loneliness is here, it is a fact of his life, and it is all too evidently going nowhere. For him, loneliness won't be curable, just as he will never get over his loss. But what keeps Bob's from tipping into chronic loneliness, which would foster a belief that the world is an inherently negative place, is his determination to keep it at a distance. And he works at it, daily. If he can do this, he suggests, anyone can.

I talk to groups of people now, mostly women because the blokes don't really turn up, but I encourage anyone who does come to one of my talks to do what I do: to volunteer, to occupy themselves by doing other things for other people. I encourage them to keep a diary, to write their own life story even, an autobiography, not necessarily to publish, but just something to leave behind for the children and the grandchildren. I've done this myself. It's kept me occupied. And that's the thing, really: keep busy. Don't give into it.

When Bob had finished writing his own memoir, entitled *Loneliness, Tell Me About It*, he had it privately published, to be distributed among his wider family. He says it was a cathartic experience, but also, perhaps inevitably, a painful one. Much as the photographs on his mantelpiece keep him in the past rather than the present, so revisiting his long married life on the page didn't exactly do much to help him move on. But in one sense, Bob doesn't want to move on. He doesn't want to forget his wife, nor the years they shared together. He wants to honour her, every day, and so by being reminded of her, by writing about her, and by talking to others about her, he keeps her alive.

And if pain comes with it, then it's worth it, he says, an unavoidable side effect. It is the pain that reminds him that he himself is still alive, and that despite it all he still has things yet to live for.

Sophie Andrews of TSL tells me that loneliness is in many ways unavoidable.

It's a phase that many of us will go through, all of us perhaps, at some point. If you are 85, and you've lost your mobility, then it's natural to feel lonely. Is it treatable? Well, what we would say is that early intervention certainly helps. It's not just about dealing with the loss of a partner, but the loss of all sorts of circumstances: your driving licence, your eyesight. The loss of a pet, the loss of mobility. Significant changes in people's lives change them; it can cast them adrift. We aim to be there for them, and we offer to put an arm around someone and be alongside them before they can get onto that slippery slope.

So, no, we don't claim to cure loneliness, but we do help to improve people's self-confidence. If you are lonely and isolated, then even talking to people every week on the telephone will, and does, help.

Many of those people, like Bob Lowe, have gone on to become volunteers themselves for TSL, and Bob is living proof of what can happen when you do make an effort, and the many positives that can come from that.

Bob reads out a section of his book for me. This passage, he explains, is about preparing a meal-for-one when cooking was never his speciality, because cooking was something his wife, a marvel in the kitchen, always took care of. In the passage, he imagines asking her about the oven temperature settings, how long the roast potatoes will need, and then he describes the pinch of pain that comes when he resolves to set the table for one, rather than for two.

'People tend to talk about loneliness as a sense of isolation, of being solitary,' he says. 'But for me, at least, it also encompasses so many other things. There is grief, despair, panic, anxiety and guilt, and all of them wrap up within loneliness.'

Since his wife died, Bob has been experiencing an ongoing sense of guilt.

I never bought Kath any flowers while she was alive, except perhaps on birthdays and Christmas. She loved flowers, but I never thought to buy them. Now she's gone, I do feel terribly guilty about that. My children tell me it's all right, that she understood. But I can't help the way I feel about it.

And so now he buys her flowers every week. The living room is filled with their scent. 'It brightens up the house,' he says. 'And it keeps her with me.'

Directory

Contact the Elderly

https://www.contact-the-elderly.org.uk/

0800 716543

FOUR

The problem with men

In being quite so open about his emotions, and so ready to talk about them on a public platform, Bob Lowe is unusual. He is unusual because he is a man, and men don't usually talk about this stuff. Though stereotyping half of humanity can only ever lead to trouble, it is nevertheless demonstrably true to suggest that men are rarely quite as capably sociable as women are. Throughout the different stages of life, we are told that it is women who are better at fostering new relationships, new friendships, at integrating themselves into new communities. If one half of a couple is more likely than the other to suggest throwing a dinner party, it is statistically more likely to be her than him.

If all this is true, and not merely the reiteration of lazy sexism, then it might explain why women continue to thrive in later age. There are more women studying at, for example, the University of the Third Age, the global peer-led initiative where people of retirement age resume their studies, not in pursuit of a degree but rather for the simple love of new learning. And also why there are far more women working within the volunteer sector. Even the average GP waiting room lacks testosterone.

The friendships that men foster throughout life – again, according to stereotype – tend to revolve around the office, the pub, football. Conversations of an emotional tenor are not always willingly entered into, and banter seems to remain the universal male shorthand (cf. Jeremy Clarkson). As one woman I talk to so succinctly puts it: 'Men tend not to talk face-to-face; they talk shoulder to shoulder.'

This is not a problem, of course, until it becomes one. When it does, what happens to these men at the point at which their working lives are over and they find, rudely, their social lives wanting? Many seem to drop off the social map altogether, retreating behind closed doors into comfortable armchairs and, over time, into themselves. But this can lead to increased vulnerability, a growing sense of isolation and, as we have seen, an ultimate descent into ill health and early death.

In Australia in the 1990s, issues around the health of men of a certain age began to circle. Australian culture, it was reported, did little to encourage men to discuss such fanciful ideas as their feelings or wellbeing, and so, as a consequence, their wellbeing began to suffer. But the collective problem was a complex one, and the solutions proffered had to be subtle and effective. This wasn't just a case of those men making an overdue appointment with the nearest medical professional. What they required even more than that, it was found, was greater social interaction. And so, in 1998, there came a new initiative to Australia: the Men's Sheds, a place where men could go to spend their retired time in a virtual recreation of the blue-collar working environment, a place of tools, sawdust and machinery. It was believed that by setting up a space in which males could gather and remain true to their already defined roles, they might also find support among one another, both on a day-to-day basis but also in times of illness, mental and physical alike.

It was hoped that such Sheds might ease the transition from full-time employment into other activities during retirement, and would provide a link between the primary health network and those who otherwise had no regular contact with the network at all. Most importantly, these men who had a surfeit of time on their hands would now be able to build themselves an environment in which they were once again made to feel welcome, a place where mutual respect and trust, perhaps even new friendships, would be paramount.

Or to put it another way, it would give them something to do with their days, their never-ending days: things to make, and do, and fix. It was a nice idea, as appealing as it was nostalgic, harking back to a time when, on those occasions when everyday items went wrong, people would get them fixed instead of simply replacing them with newer versions. So while the main activity in these sheds was whittling away at table and chair legs, they fixed cars, too. Locals would bring them their broken lawnmowers, their malfunctioning kettles. Those anglepoise lamps that hadn't switched on for years would make light again.

Simple, basic jobs well done, bringing with it the renewed pleasures of oil on fingers, and the return of days they might otherwise have feared were gone forever. The sheds were an instant success. Of course they were. They spread across the sometimes harsh, and often remote, continent, and were written about so widely, and so positively, that the initiative spread further still: to New Zealand, Ireland and the UK, and then across Europe and the US.

The first Men's Sheds in England were projects of Age UK affiliates between 2009 and 2011. The London branch opened in the north of the city, Camden, in 2011, started by a man then in his late 60s, and recently retired: Mike Jenn. By 2013, 26 other sheds opened around the country. By 2017, there were 400 nationwide. Each is autonomous and independently run and managed. They are open to anyone over the age of 50, to anyone who might want to attend, though because they meet on weekdays, they tend mostly to attract retirees and the long-term unemployed.

And, despite the name, women are permitted too, and, in some if not all cases, actively encouraged.

You don't so much stumble upon this particular Men's Shed, located in the labyrinthine backstreets of north London, as sniff out the sawdust. It is early on a Wednesday morning in an otherwise silent community centre, and the 'shed' – more a closely confined workshop, with low ceilings and strip lighting – is already a hive of activity at half past ten, half a dozen men, and one woman, already hard at work and hunched over saws and screwdrivers and chisels, each a hive of independent industriousness. There is little or no small talk; the concentration required over sharp objects doesn't permit it.

Occasionally, the kettle will whistle and someone will make a suggestion that tea's up. All the mugs are liberally chipped.

One man, tall and imposing and 70, with Father Christmas's beard and a carpenter's smock, is stooped over an ornate desk carving. 'Inspired by Moroccan design,' he informs. Another is making a chair leg to go with the other three he finished off last week. The youngest Shedder here, by several decades in fact, is a cancer survivor in his early 50s. He is crafting an improbably beautiful chessboard, its surfaces gleaming. 'One more buff,' he suggests. The buffering process making an awful racket that silences even the noise emanating from the persistent drills. When he has put the last of the finishing touches to it, and then the last after that, the evident pride he beams is hardly misplaced. Then he buffers some more.

The sole woman here, Vosjava, is doing something more artistic yet, applying the finishing touches to a series of complicated geometric wooden blocks that, when combined, create a murder of crows. 'I'm a sculptor by trade,' she tells me. I say it must be nice to be able to indulge her hobby here every Wednesday for five hours at a stretch. 'No, no,' she corrects. 'Not a hobby, a *passion*.'

Originally from Serbia, 75-year-old Vosjava is perhaps an incongruous sight within these environs. Where most of the men are like the aforementioned Father Christmas figure in his smock, or else clad in paint-splattered overalls, the sleeves of their fraying shirts rolled up to reveal pale arms and faded tattoos, Vosjava is as elegant as the avian figurines she is busy sculpting.

'I'm a sculptress without a studio, so these guys are fantastic for letting me use all this machinery,' she says. 'I'm an honorary male in this company, which is very gratifying to me.'

The machinery, and in fact all the bits and pieces here, Mike Jenn tells me, have been donated to the shed, mostly by local widows who were keen to see the tools of their late husbands' trade live on in active service. In any given shed, there are several thousand pounds worth of equipment, all similarly donated, and all of it free to use to those who turn up. That said, the sheds *are* a business, albeit in the micro sense; all run on donations. From these donations alone, Camden's shed raised close to £6,000 in 2017.

Vosjava tells me that she has been coming here for over a year. Have they all become friends, I wonder? She shakes her head. 'No, I don't know any of them privately. We are more colleagues than friends, I think. We are each in our little worlds, and we get on with our work. It is a boys' club, I would say, but I feel privileged to be a part of it.'

The sense of industry is evident. There is little laughter, but rather the collective furrowing of brows as each gets on with his or her own work. Only one man is particularly keen to talk, but in truth he is more interested in venting. He tells me he has little company during the rest of the week, and so, perhaps as a consequence, all his spleen is stored up and unleashed upon anyone who might be within earshot. To me, he talks about Brexit and immigration, the problems with gay marriage. Meanwhile, everybody else just gets on with their work. One of them, Mick, also a cancer survivor, walks from each desk in turn, as if to oversee his colleagues' efforts. Mick was once a carpenter, and so he is the de facto expert here. But his is a subtle rather than overbearing presence. He interferes in nobody's work, and only offers help when help is directly requested.

What strikes me as I watch them all work is what unifies such a disparate bunch of individuals is the collective sense of contentment. Days that had been empty are now full again;

these people have become colleagues, something that has been missing from their lives.

Mike Jenn tells me that retiring is a little like standing on the edge of a cliff, then peering over. 'It doesn't necessarily look like a good idea close-up, you know? There is too much free time, so you do need to plan for it. You need to know what you are going to do with your days, because the last thing you want is for your days to have nothing at all in them, nothing for you to do.'

Mike had had a career in project management, and was later the director of a charity. When he retired, he too wondered how he was going to fill his days.

There were lots of community activities, but they were mostly run by wives, so far as I could see. I know many men for whom retirement has become problematical. Why? Well, I suppose because their jobs identified them. They were a plumber, a carpenter. When they stopped working, they lost their sense of identity. It was very much a case of: *who am I now?*

It was Mike's son, living in Australia, who recommended he look at the Men's Shed movement. When he opened his own in 2013, he didn't quite know what to expect. Would it take off here as it had down there? There was no budget for advertising, so he simply put a couple of lines in the local paper. 'And that was all it took, really, because it took off very quickly from that. Word-of-mouth, mostly.'

The subsequent success nationwide rather perpetuated another stereotype that tends to dog males: that men, all of them, are better with brawn than brain. There is an unambiguous, and deliberately unfussy, *can-do* ethic here, and it is perhaps notable that Vosjava's artistic bent is very much overshadowed by more practical skills elsewhere. I ask Mike about those men who have no aptitude for DIY, those who don't know one screw bit from another. Because they do exist, these men.

He laughs. 'Well, I knew nothing about woodwork myself before I started all this. But guys came along, they helped one another out, and now look at me. I'm making things like... well, like this.' He holds up what was, until very recently, the trunk of a small tree. When he has finally finished carving it, it might well resemble a small stool.

'I've got a lot of similar things that I end up taking back home with me,' he says. 'My wife isn't exactly thrilled with them.'

Ability at woodcraft, he insists, is largely beside the point here. It's something more intangible than that, a male thing. 'When women get on, they arrange to meet up for a cup of coffee. But men aren't programmed that way. We are programmed to look after ourselves, irrespective of whether we actually can or not. The important thing is that we believe we can.'

Mike thinks that this is why men struggle to make lasting friendships out of the workplace. They need that common bond, something that the Men's Sheds provide. By recreating a workplace environment, that sense of workplace camaraderie – all that bluster, that Jeremy Clarkson banter, that Brexit talk – can occur in an atmosphere that feels, to its members, natural, unforced, what they always knew. They might not like everything that everyone says, but when did anyone ever like everything that everyone says?

Mike's shed is open two days a week, Tuesdays for men only, Wednesdays for both sexes. Members travel from far and wide across the city to attend. It's a small space, and so they are limited to how many people can be here at any one time – on the day I visit, a local health and safety officer arrives to assess the fire exits, and doesn't leave frowning – but the level of interest Mike fields suggests that he could easily fill this place every day of the week.

'And I imagine that if we opened on the weekends, too, we would get a very different demographic – a younger one, perhaps, people who still work but maybe don't like the work they do, or don't like their colleagues.' He smiles. 'Or maybe they just want to get away from their wives?'

Our conversation is interrupted when the cancer survivor finally finishes buffering his chessboard for the third, possibly fourth time. But its effects are evident for all to see. He holds the board up for the others to admire, which they duly do. Mick pats him on the back. 'Good work,' he says.

'The reason people come here,' Mike Jenn says, 'is for the camaraderie. They come for that sense of structure, a sense of belonging. It's like they're coming to work, and that's why they come back week after week. It gives all of us focus, I suppose, a purpose to our days. And that's what we want at any age, no? A bit of purpose, something to do.'

A week later, I catch up with Mick, the shed's resident carpentry expert. Mick Finn has been a regular face at the Camden branch for the past five years. Sixty-nine years old, he is a cancer survivor twice over: first throat cancer back in 2010, and then, in 2016, during an operation to clear a bile duct blockage, and an accompanying dose of jaundice, it was discovered that he was suffering from non-Hodgkin's lymphoma. He's had a tough few years.

'I'm not exactly in remission,' he says, his words brittle and coarse in a dry mouth that no longer produces sufficient amounts of saliva, and makes him worry whether I can understand what it is he is saying, 'but I suppose you could say I'm in the recovery stage.' He has been retired for seven years, though not necessarily willingly. 'Forced into it because, you know, the illness.'

Mick is divorced, with one grown-up son, and a couple of grandchildren. While he still worked – first as a carpenter, then a contracts manager – his social life revolved almost entirely around the pub. He was a drinker and smoker, enthusiastic in both pursuits, and would see off most nights in a local that had resisted all neighbourhood efforts to turn it into a wine bar. His local was a pub's pub, the kind that don't really exist anymore, its crepuscular light lending it a yeasty air that stirred like soup whenever anybody laughed at another off-coloured joke. When the smoking ban came in in 2007, the clientele took it badly.

'Had to go outside for a fag,' he says. 'All weathers.'

The cancer diagnosis, when it came, proved to be that most humdrum of things: an inevitable surprise. 'The doctor told me that if I wanted to live, I'd have to make drastic lifestyle changes.' And so, overnight, his social life as he knew it was obliterated. 'I was housebound, but enforced, you know? I couldn't carry on like that, I couldn't go back to the pub, and so it all just – well, it stopped. I didn't see most of them, my mates, again.'

Such an abrupt end to that life hit him hard. At first, he tried to convince himself that he could remain a regular, and merely avoid drinking alcohol while there. 'Easy enough to say, I'll have a Coke, but it doesn't work that way. The temptation, you see? I wasn't just a normal drinker.'

Though he refuses to recognise it himself – his drinking, he says, never interfered with his work – his doctor told him that his habit had bordered on alcoholism. 'The quantity I used to drink, the doctor said, was very, very excessive. So I had no choice but to stay as far away from the pub as possible.' He shrugs. 'But what was I supposed to do now?'

He struggled. He was assigned a social worker, and one day the social worker suggested he might attend something called a Lunch Club, a local neighbourhood initiative that gathered people together for a sit-down meal. There would be bingo to follow, shortly after dessert had been cleared away. But, Mick says, 'I just thought: no, no, no. *Bingo?* With a bunch of old people? Nah. Not me. Never played bingo in my life, mate. Why would I start now?'

His social worker then found out about the Men's Shed, and quickly realised this might be more Mick's thing. It was. 'I went down there one day, and I've been going ever since.' Mick is a permanent presence there every Tuesday and Wednesday. If it ran five days a week, he'd be there every day. 'Weekends too, because what else am I going to do? I like being there. It keeps me busy. And if I can help other people, I feel useful again.'

It has also given him something he thought he might never get again this late in life: a new, *proper* friend.

There's this one particular bloke I hit it off with. He doesn't come down to the sheds anymore, but we still do meet once a week. We've got pretty much the same outlook on life, see? So we go to things like craft shows, antique fairs. One day, he might pop down and see me, have a cup of tea, or I go to him, exactly the same. What do we chat about? We chat about life in general. It's an outlet.

On warmer days, they might head down to a nearby reservoir that has been turned into wetlands. This is where Mick can indulge another recent pastime, photography. He photographs insects, and the wildlife that makes the ponds their home. It passes the time. And if life is hard when you live alone on the eve of your 70th birthday, still riddled with health issues, then you need all the plugs you can get. The alternative doesn't bear thinking about.

'Sometimes I see my old mates down Camden, coming out of the pub after a session, and I think to myself, I think: *God, that used to be me!* So my illness has been a bit of a godsend, I suppose you could say.'

Like everyone else in the Men's Sheds, Mick has made an awful lot of furniture. Some of the items he keeps, others he gives away. Some are sold in flea markets and car boot sales to help with the ongoing fundraising efforts to keep the sheds viable. But what gives him most pleasure, he confesses, is watching everyone else at work, offering help when they need it, and simple encouragement when they are perfectly capable of working by themselves.

A week earlier, I had watched him methodically weave his way around the workbenches, this benevolent gaffer, the old lag, the one to whom everyone glances to check they are doing the right thing. 'No fingers have been lost on my watch yet,' he'd smiled.

It is in this place that he has found his new community. 'We look out for one another here, you know? If somebody doesn't turn up one day, we ring up to find out where they are, if they're okay. Once, when I was in hospital, a couple of the lads even came down to see me, to see how I was doing.' He stops to clear his throat before continuing. 'That was unexpected. It was nice of them. I appreciated it.'

Directory
Men's Sheds
http://menssheds.org.uk/
0300 772 9626

FIVE

The mental health benefits of tea and scones

In 1965, while still a university student, future lawyer Trevor Lyttleton encountered a couple of his elderly neighbours in the street one day. He was living in Marylebone at the time, an area that was in the midst of vigorous upmarket regeneration, the redevelopment of townhouses dwarfing the already fading council blocks behind it. But the inhabitants of those council blocks, he realised, were getting left behind in its facelift, rendered invisible and largely forgotten. He mentioned to friends that it was a shame they didn't get out so much anymore, and it appeared to him they had precious few people left to talk to.

'I suggested to these friends that we might take them out one afternoon. I mean, why not? I thought it might be a giggle,' he says to me.

A few weeks later, they did just that, and a bunch of them, in cars, took the neighbourhood's lonely older folk on a day trip to Hampton Court. They chose a Sunday, because even in 1965 Sunday was viewed, for some, as the saddest day. A spirit of adventure was in the air as they set off, but it was only once they were on their way that the full ramifications of his simple act of kindness began fully to dawn.

'We-ll,' he says, drawing one syllable into two, 'it was a bit of a rocky start, I suppose, because there were quite a number of, shall we say, *characters* within the group. But over the course of the day, the exchanges between them all became increasingly moving, and I began to realise the value of what we were doing here.'

It was clear that the old people, alone for much of their week, valued the sudden connection highly, not just with their own peer group but with people so much younger than themselves. They came back to life, revived. By day's end, firm friendships were cemented amidst promises to keep in touch. 'Not everybody had telephones in those days, so we watched as they all exchanged addresses. All said they'd love to do something like this again, so I knew that we had stumbled upon something.'

Lyttleton's unwitting philanthropy was unusual. Here was a young man on the brink of a successful career, and in the midst of a decade just beginning to realise that decadence was to be its defining characteristic. So what on earth was he, Lyttleton, doing by directing his efforts towards people so deep into later life, and attempting to lighten their load?

Lots of reasons, he says. His studies at the time were focusing around the importance of something called unit trusts, 'which I hated, actually.' The main reason his interests had been so piqued by the old people he passed each day on Marylebone's grey pavements was more personal. 'I had grown up with this amazing Welsh grandmother of mine. She was mischievous and cultivated, and such an interesting woman. I used to visit her a lot, and I loved spending time with her.'

School friends had mocked him for spending so much of his free time with her when he could be spending it with people his own age. 'I simply said to them that *she* was far more interesting than they were. She used to read racy books; she had a wicked sense of humour. Really, she was tirelessly entertaining, and I adored her.'

These current neighbours of his, then, reminded him of his grandmother. Being kind to them was his way of honouring her memory. 'I have to say that at first I thought we were doing them all a tremendous favour, lifting their horizons and so on,' he admits. He confesses, too, that he didn't necessarily expect to do it all again, much less make it a regular occasion. 'But it was explained to me by a friend that if I had started taking them out, then I could hardly simply stop, could I? Eradicating the loneliness for a single afternoon would only amplify it if I simply then disappeared from their lives.'

So the outings became a bit of a thing. Soon, he was managing demand. He enrolled more volunteers, and placed an advert in *The Times* – 'Have fun helping the old,' the ad ran – and in magazines. The responses were swift, and many. But some were puzzling. 'We were called, simply, "Contact" back then, and after we placed an advert in Michael Heseltine's *About Town* magazine, we started getting some very strange phone calls at the office…'

About Town, it transpired, was also running an advert for something else called Contact, but this was for an altogether different form of human connection: wife swapping. The phone calls that flooded in brought blood to cheeks, and were swiftly redirected. 'We quickly changed our name to "Contact the Elderly", largely to spare us any further blushes,' he laughs.

Lyttleton did go on to become a successful lawyer, but he also flexed his artistic muscle by writing and composing music for the theatre. Meanwhile, Contact the Elderly (CtE) was sprouting wings. They had one group in the first year, two by the second, four by year three, and 11 groups 12 months after that. At first, the outings went far and wide, but over the years the roads got busier, the petrol more expensive. They decided instead to host tea parties in willing participants' houses up and down the country. There were many willing participants. If the local elderly weren't mobile themselves, others volunteered to drive them.

It was, and remains, a charmingly sweet idea, but Lyttleton could have had little clue to just how much his eureka moment would endure. Six decades later, the charity is still thriving. Though it employs a small staff of just 40, it now has over 11,000 volunteers nationwide, who between them host 800 tea parties a month.

'In 2013, the government described the fact of there being nearly two million elderly people off the radar as a national disgrace,' he says.

But there remains no real initiative to tackle it. It is simply not being dealt with properly within government. But if relatives continue to abdicate responsibility, or move away, then more and more old people will be left alone, and lonely. So I'm grateful that so many people volunteer for us today, but to be honest with you, we are just scraping the surface of what is a vast problem.

Now in his 70s, Lyttleton continues to lobby government for tangible change. In 2011, he received an MBE for services to the elderly, an honour which merely proved to be grist to his mill. He writes a lot of letters, and addresses a great many of them to incumbent prime ministers, and to members of Parliament, urging in everyone awareness, and urging action.

'And I'll tell you one thing,' he says, finger wagging. 'I don't intend to stop.'

At a little after 2 o'clock on the first Sunday of November, Elizabeth Amodu is preparing her modest living room for the imminent arrival of today's guests. She tells me she isn't quite sure how many people will turn up. 'Maybe five, perhaps as many as 10. But some, I think, are ill, so they won't be here.' Some she has met before, others she will be encountering for the first time. Two sofas have been pushed against the far walls, while chairs from the kitchen have been brought in and arranged in a semicircle for those who might prefer sitting in a more upright position.

In the corner is a table upon which sits the kind of understated feast you might see at any children's party: white bread sandwiches with the crusts cut off, alongside an array of sundry cakes and scones erupting with whipped cream and strawberry jam. Her husband, Taiwo, is boiling the kettle for tea and coffee, son Temi busy watching cartoons on television.

Elizabeth has been hosting Contact the Elderly parties for the past couple of years. 'But I only manage maybe twice a year, which I do feel guilty about.' She smiles shyly. 'I want to do more. I *should* do more!'

The people she is about to host nevertheless have fairly busy social lives, convening as they do at events like this once a month at other houses in the area. If Elizabeth is too busy to host them, then there are many others willing to step in. Elizabeth and her family are originally from Nigeria, and settled in the UK a decade ago. She is a tutor, teaching computers to the elderly at a nearby college, and her husband is an engineer. Temi, seven, attends the local school.

'Where I come from, ladies like to dress up and go to a party,' she says. A youthful 48 years old, Elizabeth is a sweetly vivacious woman, full of life. Her smile is an act of grace. 'They don't go to eat food, they go to chat, to get up and dance, to be in company. And I think the people here are the same: nobody comes for the food, not really. They come to be with each other.' She says that she loves hosting these events, 'because I like the idea of giving back. I like to help people. It's part of my culture.'

When she and her husband first arrived in the UK, Elizabeth was keen to do charity work. In Nigeria, she says, it is important to do charitable things, to give back to society whenever possible. In the UK, she has completed sponsored runs for cancer charities, and even though she teaches computer skills to members of the older generation, she wants to do more for them. 'Coming to this country, I found I missed my parents a lot, so to have elderly people coming to our house, it feels like a good thing to do.'

Her home is located within a quiet council estate on the fringes of south-east London, with views of tower blocks and parking spaces. The criteria for volunteers hosting tea parties is simple: no (or very few) steps up to the front door, and a downstairs toilet for quick and easy access. Elizabeth's has both.

The doorbell rings its sonorous chimes, and Taiwo goes to greet the first arrivals: Harry, Audrey and Peggy, and their volunteer driver, Steve. A few minutes later, it rings again. Maureen, Magna, Jean. Coats and walking sticks are put to one side, and everyone congregates in the front room. Elizabeth begins to hand out the sandwiches, Temi the fat ripe purple grapes on toothpicks. Taiwo bustles into the room with a teapot, and won't take no for an answer. It is 3 o'clock.

'I've been waiting to come here since midday,' Peggy tells me. Peggy is in her late 80s. She is thin-lipped, rigid in her posture, and her forehead is concertina'd into an impressively severe frown, the two tramlines that meet between the eyebrows like italicised quotation marks. 'Hate Sundays,' she says. 'Just hate them. The worst days.' Peggy's late husband, Sid, a pilot in World War II, died eight years ago. She confesses that she has been miserable ever since. 'And so the sooner I join him, the better.'

Tania, one of CtE's volunteers and a woman with a naturally bright disposition, her smile spilling from her eyes and lighting up the air around her, attempts to cajole Peggy towards a better mood, but fails.

'I always tell them,' Tania says to me later, 'that they can bring their gripes with them, but that they must try to focus on more positive things while they are here, if only for their own sake.' She laughs brightly. 'Doesn't always work, though...'

Gripping my arm, and pulling me in close, Peggy tells me that she had three children. One died in a climbing accident a decade ago. The two that remain are scattered around the country, busy with their own lives. 'I hardly get to see my grandchildren.' We talk about how she fills her days, and she talks about the various clubs and committees of which she is a member. She is a member of many. She sounds too busy to be lonely, I say to her, but she suggests otherwise. After we have been speaking for almost half an hour, she looks up to see everyone else engaged in their own conversations around her.

Her frown deepens. 'See how they all talk amongst themselves?' She slurps from her tea and begins the slow, but steady, process of warming up.

Later, I will see her smile. I will see her laugh.

Across the room is the only man here today, Harry. Harry is 93. He tells me that another man, Frank, used to come to these occasions, but not any more. He is not really sure why. Harry has dressed up for today's tea party, pressed suit and tie, and, on his lapel, what looks like a war medal. I mean to ask about it, but get distracted and forget. He reaches for his jacket's breast pocket, and brings out a photograph of his late wife to show me. It is yellowed around the edges, and fraying slightly. Tania, appearing suddenly at his shoulder, promises to laminate it for him, 'so that the fraying won't get any worse.'

Peering at me through cloudy eyes behind heavily framed glasses, the lenses of which are so dusty I want to polish them for him, Harry tells me about his life, the consequences of outliving your spouse, and the reduction of his social life as a result. He talks fondly about his four-year-old Rottweiler, a guard dog in stature but a puppy in demeanour, and talks also of his youngest daughter, with whom he is currently residing. She is in her 50s, he says, and has just survived breast cancer. 'She's not working at the moment. She's always out with friends. I hardly ever see her.'

At one point in the afternoon, Noush, another volunteer, announces that, like last year, they will be doing Secret Santa again. Tania hoots, and claps joyfully. With just seven weeks until Christmas, Noush says, it's time to make preparations. She passes out handmade, personalised Christmas cards to everyone in turn, inside of which is the name of the person they will be buying a present for. Peggy complains that she can't get out of the house, so someone will have to buy the present on her behalf. Tania, the kind of person we all need in our lives, readily volunteers. Harry, because of what he calls a 'botched' cataract operation, can't quite make out his card. He asks me to read it for him.

'Ho ho ho,' I recite. '*It's Secret Santa time again. This year you are buying a present for* _____' And here I whisper the recipient's name.

Harry nods uncomprehendingly, looks up at me, looks back at the card, then again at me. 'I can't read it,' he says. 'Who have I got to buy for?'

I whisper the name again.

'Who?'

Louder this time, I whisper again: '*Magna.*'

He turns to me. 'I can't hear you.'

By now, I am practically shouting. '*MAGNA!*'

He sits back in his chair, and blinks slowly. 'Magna? Which one's Magna?'

At 99 years old, Joan is the oldest member of the group. A former teacher, she retired four full decades ago, and until fairly recently spent a highly satisfying retirement travelling the world with her now late husband, who had also been a teacher.

'America, Scandinavia, France,' she says, counting off the destinations on her fingers. She has borne widowhood better than most, and remains alert, and alive in the figurative sense of the word. She is the most delightful company. Though she now has considerable mobility problems – the walking frame in the corner is hers – she tells me that she retains a rapacious interest in the world, and the people, around her.

'I'm lucky, because I like to read a lot. So even though I can't really get out of the house very much anymore, I can still do that. I can still read. That keeps the boredom at bay.'

Having worked her way through pretty much the entire canon of Victorian novels, and confessing little appetite for modern fiction, she is currently reading post-war biographies. 'I'm fascinated by how people lived, and rebuilt their lives, after the war.' She is intrigued, too, by Trump, and by what 'sensible Americans' must make of him.

As we chat literature and politics, Magna watches on. Magna, who is in her 70s, tells me that Jean is an amazing woman, an inspiration to them all. 'To have your health at her age is a wonderful thing.'

Joan agrees. 'Oh, I've no doubt been very lucky indeed.' She taps a crooked finger on her temple. 'I've still got all my marbles. No hair anymore, mind you.' This is true. Aside from a cloud of wispy white hair that curls itself around the back of her head and ears, she is quite bald. '… But I still have my marbles.'

One of the realities of groups like this is that members die off fairly frequently; their numbers become steadily depleted. Several of the men have gone recently, and though death at their age is more inevitable than it is for younger generations – everyone here is a veteran of funerals – each passing is keenly mourned over. They are all familiar with widowhood already; to then see members of their own group diminish seems somehow even more tauntingly cruel.

But Tania, whose glass is always half full if not perennially spilling over, is already looking forward to, and busy planning, Joan's 100th birthday celebrations. As Taiwo serves more tea, and Temi more cake, Tania talks about the telegram from the Queen that will come, and discusses potential locations for the party they will throw. The occasion is still nine long months away, but everybody promises to be there.

'It will be on a Saturday,' Tania says, turning to me. 'You're more than welcome to come.'

Directory

Contact the Elderly

https://www.contact-the-elderly.org.uk/

0800 716543

SIX

A room with a view

Melissa Lawrence has lived in the same house in the same New Jersey neighbourhood for her entire life. She is 24 years old. For the last 12 months, since developing an array of complicated health issues, she has rarely left the four walls of the family home.

'I'm here five days of the week,' she says. 'I don't go out.'

At the weekends, she does make small concessions towards the wider world, largely to appease her parents: a couple of hours' shopping on Saturday mornings; an early trip to a nearby church on Sunday. If, after the service, they can find a suitably vegan-friendly restaurant for Melissa, they might grab a quick green lunch before heading back. But such ventures into the outside world drain her, and so these weekends are spent decompressing after the morning's tiresome exertions.

Though she doesn't particularly like labels – considers them unhelpful and, often, misguided – Melissa thinks she might be NEET. I tell her I have not come across NEET before, and so she endeavours to explain. 'It stands for Not in Education, Employment or Training.' There are growing numbers of

NEETs all over the world, I learn. According to Wikipedia – and corroborated elsewhere – there are now over half a million NEETs in Australia, accounting for one in eight Australians between the ages of 15 and 29. There are almost a million NEETs in the UK, and as a generational affliction it seems particularly prevalent in the US. One proffered reason is the fallout from the 2008 global recession. The world has become an unforgiving, even hostile place. More and more of us want to take refuge from it, to hide.

Melissa also thinks she might be part-hikikomori. Hikikomori I do know about: it's that Japanese term to describe those individuals who actively withdraw from all societal interaction. According to one doctor I speak to, 'it connotes the idea of a constellation of systems coming together, and together painting a portrait of a problem, a mental health problem.'

Hikikomori arguably represents the very apogee of social isolation, and is sufficiently widespread across Japan that its government has taken note. Hikikomori are a discernible demographic, and those that are afflicted are people who haven't left their homes for more than six months, and who exist, and interact, with the wider world largely via the internet. They otherwise avoid social contact wherever possible; the only fully three-dimensional people they do come into regular contact with are family members, with whom they often continue to live.

'We do know that mental health conditions are complex,' says the aforementioned doctor. 'This is why we don't have a perfect understanding of what causes this particular condition yet, because a whole litany of conditions cause it. The brain is complicated. Human beings are complicated. And so of course *hikikomori* is complicated.'

If being *hikikomori* requires the enabling of dutiful, concerned, parents, then it is also clearly facilitated by the presence of modern technology. One wouldn't have been able to be *hikikomori* before the internet age; if they had had comparable conditions – and of course a great many people did – they would have withdrawn more fully, and interacted much less. They would have been labelled depressed, agoraphobic. But the internet allows them to continue to exist in the world, even if that very suggestion – 'to live' – requires the employment of quotation marks.

Melissa Lawrence first came across the term in one of the anime cartoons she used to watch on Saturday morning TV. 'I never saw it being talked about very much in the Western world,' she tells me when we speak via Skype one early New Jersey morning, 'but I saw it referred to in Japanese shows a lot.' She looked up the word afterwards, and saw that it meant 'pulling in', 'introverted'.

'And that really resonated with me. I recognised it in myself.'

I watch her as she talks to me, sitting on a sofa in her room. There is a window over her left shoulder, in which low clouds gather. She is young and slim, with long brown hair. She is pretty and chatty and personable, and laughs a lot, and easily. She does not seem to me particularly withdrawn. While we speak, she makes full eye contact and talks in long, flowing, grammatically correct sentences. She strikes me as very present, and highly mentally alert. Not what I would have expected from someone who, to all intents and purposes, was deliberately removing herself from so much of the tangible human race.

Yes, she agrees in concession, but speaking to people via technology, even when the subject might stray into highly personal territory, is fine for her. She is happy with it, used to it. She believes that were we to have this conversation face-to-face, and not through a computer screen, it might become more problematical for her. 'There might be an undercurrent of awkwardness. But like this, on Skype, it's fine. I'm comfortable.'

I tell her I'm interested in what it must be like to withdraw from the analogue world, and to live digitally. What, I ask her, constitutes a typical day?

She seems to like this question. She sits forward, and smiles. 'Okay. Well, I get up at about 7.30, 8 o'clock, and come downstairs to eat breakfast. And then, at around 8.30, I start focusing on my book.'

Though she had previously labelled herself as NEET, Melissa is actually anything but. She is a writer. She self-published a novel, *The Autumnal Winds*, in mid-2017, and at the end of that year followed it up with a book of poetry, co-authored with her Taiwanese boyfriend Cheng-Wei Lien, called *Taiwan: Hearts Beating with Love*.

'Then, from about 9 o'clock until 11, I might talk to my boyfriend in Taiwan, or some other friends online, and I journal a lot. Someone once gave me some very good advice: to keep a journal. He said that it would make me feel better. And he was right.'

She holds up a hardbacked, ornately designed diary for me to see. 'I love my journal, it's beautiful! So, yes, I spend my morning

journalling, and then I have lunch, and then in the afternoon…
Well, I used to paint a lot, but I got bored of that. I was doing
watercolour, and watercolour is very hard to manipulate. Then
I got interested in a Japanese threading technique. You use silk
thread…' She holds up a packet of the silk thread to the camera.
'… But I haven't started that yet because I don't know how to
do it!' She laughs, and shyly covers her mouth with a hand. 'I
thought that maybe I could make some bracelets for people?
But it's complicated…

'So anyway, yes, the rest of my day. I tend to do random art
stuff in the afternoon, and then maybe watch a bit of TV with
my mom. Dinner is early, at about 4 o'clock, and from 5 until
6.30, I speak with my friend in Australia about philosophy and
current events. That's like a meeting of minds!'

And the evenings?

'In the evenings, I like to watch Japanese documentaries,
often with my father, because I love all things Japan, and
watching TV shows about it makes me feel as if I am actually
there. Then maybe a little bit more TV, and I'm in bed by 9,
10 o'clock.'

This all sounds, to me, like the pursuit of a highly organised
life in miniature. She is a hive of activity, of productivity. And
so, as such, Melissa is succeeding. She has everything she
needs around her: the love and understanding of her parents,
an ongoing healthy vegan diet, friends across the world, and
unlimited broadband. She calls home her 'safe haven', and
seems perfectly content.

But any safe haven must be a protection against something
more hostile. She admits that she feels far less safe outside, in

what feels to her like an unpredictable, and often harsh, world. Out there, life has less structure, and can be full of unwanted surprises. She doesn't much crave unwanted surprises.

'Life outside is much more complicated and scary,' she says.

It turns out that she might have good reason to feel this way.

In 2016, Melissa, an otherwise fairly healthy young woman, was diagnosed with a number of interconnecting health problems. There was the complicated back problem affecting the lower spine, which may well have been the result of having had scoliosis as a child. She developed a skin condition which made her itch a lot, and the repetitive scratching caused another skin condition. She also has flat feet, and requires special shoes. Walking even comparatively short distances tires her out.

Increasingly bewildered by this litany of ailments, she went to see her doctor. 'I was feeling lethargic, but I thought that it was maybe hormonal, women's problems or something. But then the doctor found a lump on my neck.'

A biopsy later confirmed the doctor's fears. 'I was diagnosed with papillary thyroid cancer. So there's that as well now,' she says.

Melissa wondered how this could happen. She really was otherwise pretty healthy. She was a vegan. She didn't drink, didn't smoke. So why, how? The doctor suggested it might have been the result of contaminants, or else everyday New Jersey pollution. The good news was that the lump was small, the size of a pea, and slow-growing. But whoever heard of a doctor that didn't want to operate? She suggested a thyroidectomy.

'They wanted to cut it open, and get it out,' Melissa clarifies. Which seemed like the most effective course of action, but she was against it. 'I just thought that it would cause even more health problems.'

A cancer specialist agreed to respect her wishes, and enrolled her into their so-called Wait and See Program. Every six months, she gets another MRI scan. If the cancer grows, they will operate; if it doesn't, they will cede to her wishes and pursue instead traditional Chinese herbs from a traditional Chinese medicine doctor.

I'm 24 years old, and I think to myself: how could I have all these health problems? It's not fair. You know, I grew up trying to be a good person, studying, trying to get all the A's, the A+'s. So why is this all happening to me? I ask myself this all the time, but then I try hard not to, because if I think about it too much – well, it gets me sad.

Dr Alan Teo is a psychiatrist and faculty member at the Oregon Health & Science University. Like all doctors, he is intrigued by the unusual cases, the ones he can learn from, and so his specialised area has become working with patients suffering from extreme forms of social isolation. Hikikomori might have originated in Japan, but there are now many such cases right across the world.

'Every month,' he tells me, 'I get emails from concerned family members telling me they think one of their children might be hikikomori.'

He believes the causes are due to psychological and social factors, along with social context. For example, there are features of the Japanese culture in terms of its family structure, and communication within that unit, that render the relationship between mother and child particularly protective, even swaddling. 'And so some of these factors can heighten the risk of hikikomori.'

So when a child withdraws into themselves, the parent's — particularly the mother's, says Dr Teo — instinct is to enable that withdrawal, and to further protect them. The enabling is essentially a proponent of the condition: by continuing to provide for the child, and by feeding them regularly, and by doing their washing, they need never come out of their bedroom, should they not want to.

'If we were living in Mongolia, in a communal tent, all under one roof and in the same room, you simply couldn't have hikikomori; it couldn't occur,' he says. 'Everyone is right in front of each other all the time, with no physical ability to isolate. But Japan has reached economic development where children are able to have their own world.'

And many of them retreat into that world.

In America, meanwhile, doctors have seen the rise and rise of what has been called 'basement dwellers', i.e., young adults, often male and over the age of 18, but still living under their parents' roof, in their basements, where the only avenue in life they fully explore is the playing of videogames. These basement dwellers are also NEET. 'This isn't quite hikikomori,' Dr Teo says, 'but you can see similar symptoms.'

But the symptoms nevertheless remain vague. And so, given that it is not the same as agoraphobia, but neither is it schizophrenia (though there are prevalent psychiatric issues), how does one go about treating it?

'Well, it's complicated. Because if we treat the social anxiety disorder, that doesn't necessarily mean *case closed*. And so we need to pay more attention to the issues surrounding the social isolation and the loneliness.'

In other words, why *do* people seek to perpetuate such a state?

Yes, precisely. Humans evolved as a social species. We evolved under social conditions that include face-to-face contact, with family members, friends, people you call your kin. That's how we evolved. And we know that it acts as an antidote to depression. Hikikomori occurs when we no longer seek such interaction. But it takes time. It doesn't happen overnight.

If it takes time to develop, it also takes time to 'cure'. At some level, the doctor says,

... the treatment is still in the Wild West. Because we don't know; we don't know what works yet. We have community-based providers in Japan who will be offering different types of talk therapy, but there haven't been studies yet that give us a systematic look into objectively comparing treatments, or knowing how best to respond to people with the condition. We have lots of potential solutions, but no firm data yet.

It's a work in progress, then.

In her high school years, Melissa Lawrence attended her local private Catholic school. It was large and rambling, and held over 1500 students. It proved the perfect place to get lost in the crowd. Melissa did.

'I didn't make many friends there, and I guess I didn't really enjoy it,' she says. 'After high school, we all moved on, and lost touch with each other. I don't actually have many friends in real life at all, but I do online.' While her three-dimensional peer group may have failed her, their internet counterparts have not. 'Oh, they support me in everything I do, and everything I'm going through! They are here for me, always, and I really, really appreciate that.' She tells me about one online friend in California who recently sent her a care package full of stickers and things she liked. 'I was really happy about that.'

To date, she hasn't met any of her online friends, and it seems she is happy, or at least accepting, that she might never. Perhaps it's easier not to meet them. Why complicate matters? She says she would like to meet her Taiwanese boyfriend, but that isn't easy, either. An electronic engineer, he is keen to travel to America, and to stay and work there, but the immigration laws are convoluted. 'And,' she points out, 'very expensive.'

So in the meantime, she remains marooned in her room, in her house. Her mother tells her regularly that she prays for her, that she hopes she gets better, and that she manages to get out into the world one day and find herself a job. Melissa did have a job last year, in a Chinese takeaway, but tells me that it wasn't for her. 'I quit after, like, two days.' When she announced to her parents that she wanted to write a book, her father gave her six months to indulge her creative itch.

When she not only wrote the book, but had it published, he was quietly impressed. I ask her whether he has read it yet, and she smiles and blushes. 'No, I don't think so. But he did send a copy to his mother, my grandmother, 500 miles away in Pennsylvania.'

She doesn't know if her grandmother has read it yet, either. She says she is embarrassed to ask.

'Since my cancer diagnosis, my dad isn't pushing me to get a job any more. I think he's just trying to make sure I'm happy. He tells me jokes, and keeps me occupied. If a deer walks through our garden, he'll point it out. He tries to keep me engaged.'

And despite her many restrictions, Melissa does indeed remain very highly engaged. She reads a lot, she writes, and composes poetry. She looks forward to her nightly Skype calls with her Australian friend. Talking about philosophy, she suggests, expands her mental horizons.

I talk to a lot of my friends about a lot of things. Sometimes they say to me that they are looking forward to spending time with me, which I assume means that they are lonely, too, but then that's an issue people tend to skirt around, I think. There is definitely a disconnect in this generation. Everyone is glued to their phones, but I think we've lost that human element: touching; the sense of touch. Hugging someone, shaking hands. You miss that on Skype, on the internet. But then, you know, the internet is also good because it allows us to connect to people all over the world. For example, I have a friend in Indonesia, so I am learning all about Indonesian culture. I have friends in China, in Taiwan, and they teach me stuff I wouldn't have otherwise learned. So there are pros and cons to everything, right?

On those rare hours Melissa does save on electricity bills, and ventures out – her Saturday morning expeditions with her parents, Sunday mornings to church – she tends to find them overwhelming. She no longer likes being in large crowds. When confronted with one, she narrows her field of vision: the aisles in the shops, the products on the shelves. She does this until she has blocked everything else out. 'It makes it easier to cope.' She stares down at her feet. She breathes deeply. She cannot wait until she is home again, to decompress, to recoup. To hide.

I ask her whether she has ever sought a cure for her condition, whether she has ever spoken to a psychiatrist perhaps? She shakes her head. 'No, but writing in my journal helps. My journal is like my best friend; she doesn't judge me.'

Where does she see herself in five years' time? Will she still be inside the house, or does she hope to have re-joined the world? She thinks for a while before answering. 'Because of my health problems, I'm just taking it one day at a time.'

Things could be worse, she points out. She has arranged her life in manageable ways. She is not festering. She is rarely bored. I ask if she is happy?

A few moments of ruminative silence, then: 'Um, no, I guess I'm not. I don't know why all this is happening to me. It doesn't seem fair. But, look, I'm not trying to waste away here. I like to gather knowledge. It is my job now to gather information and knowledge from people, and then to learn and share my knowledge with others. I try to learn a new thing every day. I'm not wasting away.'

Every day, she browses Wikipedia, looking things up, learning new nuggets of information, some profound, others less so. The previous day, she looked up pigs. 'Did you know that there are over one billion pigs on earth right now?' She laughs loudly. 'That's a lot of pigs, right?'

After we speak, the Skype sessions will continue: she has friends in London, in Poland. She probably has friends in New Jersey itself, people who might never become fully real to her, un-pixelated, but will instead remain online. At some point, Melissa might seek help, a cure, because help is out there. But she needs to be ready for it, and for perfectly good and sane reasons, she isn't ready quite yet.

'Obviously, there is a sense of loneliness and longing,' she will admit, 'because I can't be together with my friends, and sometimes I do want to be with them. I want to play board games, dominoes, Monopoly. Or maybe I want to go to the library with them; to a special event. But I can't. I can't imagine having been hikikomori pre-internet age because of that lack of social contact. There was no Skype, no social media, no texting. Imagine! That would have been hard, I think. So I'm thankful that the internet does exist.'

The last thing she says particularly stays with me.

Sometimes, if I see an aeroplane out of the window, I think, 'I wish I could be on it. I wish I could travel.' You know how humans have a sense of *wanderlust* inside them? They want to see and explore new places, new things? Well, I have that innate feeling inside my heart, too. It's there.

Directory

Contact a psychiatrist or psychologist if you are concerned about yourself or someone you care about having *hikikomori*. Psychotherapists with expertise in social anxiety may be of assistance in some cases. In addition, updated information on *hikikomori* and resources may be available on Dr Teo's webpage at http://DrAlanTeo.com/

SEVEN

The baby blues

After a few protractedly unpleasant weeks of trying, and failing, to cross its caramel-scented threshold, Michelle Kennedy began to develop an almost pathological fear towards her local Starbucks. This was awkward for her for many reasons, chief among them the simple fact that she liked her coffee, even Starbucks coffee. The problem, however, wasn't its signature latte.

'I'd see all these other mums in there, just hanging around together, their babies asleep in their arms while they were chatting away, and I would think to myself: why can't I do that?'

Michelle, back then very new to motherhood, was never able to sit still with her baby, Finn. Finn was what so many babies, to so many new parents, can occasionally seem: a tyrant, albeit a pint-sized one, with a list of non-verbal demands as long as his patience was short. Finn would only ever settle if his mother remained perpetually on the move, power-walking behind the pram up the steep inclines of her neighbourhood. And so, for the first few months of his life, he saw an awful lot of its steep inclines. His mother, meanwhile, adrift in that highly distinctive oasis of maternity leave, couldn't get the image of Starbucks, or its largely female clientele bathing in its soft-armchaired comfort, out of her head. Being on the outside looking in left her with a sour feeling.

Why, she wanted to know, were they getting on so well with each other, and how had they met? Was there any way she could infiltrate the group, and become friends with them? 'There is nothing more isolating,' she states, 'than when you see what you perceive to be the perfect friendships everywhere, all around you, but those that are excluding you, and leaving you on the outside. I was on the outside.'

Were you to come across Michelle Kennedy for the first time, you might come away convinced that she was one of those idealised Starbucks mothers: full of the quiet self-contentment of people very much in control of their situation, and 'perfect' in the way that some new mothers – though never those of your own acquaintance, curiously – can sometimes seem to be. She was young (30 at the time), attractive, nice clothes, even better hair, and professionally successful. She had a professionally successful husband, a house in an enviable part of London, a big car in the drive, and her career was on the rise. A former corporate lawyer who went on to become deputy CEO of Badoo, the online European dating platform, motherhood might have seemed like merely the last piece of the jigsaw to complete the unimprovable picture.

In private moments, she might have felt similarly herself.

But then I had Finn, and suddenly everything was really, really hard. I don't know why I didn't expect it, but I didn't. We are taught, initially, to focus on ourselves and our own ambitions, aren't we? We are told to do well at school, get your grades, a good degree, a good job. And we do our best to do just that. But then, when you have a baby, you suddenly find that there are no real goals anymore, not really. You're just adrift, somehow. And it's all new. And there is no way of knowing whether you are doing a good job or not. With motherhood, I found it all completely overwhelming. But I didn't want to tell anyone I was struggling, because that would have felt like a failure, and I was already feeling like a failure – because I didn't have a natural birth.

Her baby had been too big, and Michelle's hips too narrow. Caesarean, in this case, wasn't so much the fashionable option as the only option, the necessary one. But to her, this constituted failure. Worse was to come. 'I couldn't get him to feed, couldn't get him to sleep. To be honest, I had no idea what I was doing.'

Meanwhile, her world had shrunk drastically. She had stopped going out, stopped seeing friends, and failed to make new ones. 'I lost weight, cried all the time. I felt – and this was despite the presence of my in-laws, and my lovely mother – completely and utterly alone.'

As she says this, from the vantage point of four years down the line, the recollection throws tramlines across her forehead. The memory, she admits, brings it all flooding back, 'just the most overwhelming sense of hopelessness.'

The idea of early parenthood is sold to us upon a lie. No one ever suggests it's easy, of course, but then no one tells us quite how hard it will be, either. The hard part lies behind a veil of secrecy beyond which all new parents necessarily cower, erroneously convinced that everyone else is doing it far better than they. There are presumably many reasons for this subterfuge, but mostly it seems that no one wants to be seen to be flailing in so fundamentally biological a role, or such a seemingly instinctive one.

The image often portrayed of early motherhood is of smiling babies in highchairs being spoonfed gloop in primary colours while Mummy wafts around the kitchen in cotton that has just been Persil'd, or baby cooing itself to sleep in a designer cot while a rotating mobile lulls it towards another unbroken 10-hour sleep. Whenever a more realistic picture is painted – the spoonfed gloop has been discourteously upended all over the floor by a newly made human several months away from even grasping the basic concepts of decorum, and the Persil-soft cotton has sick stains on it – it comes delivered via the medium of sitcom. Laughter in the dark is always permitted, but best not to dwell upon it too much afterwards, yes?

If we want a more accurate picture of the bloody battle that is early parenthood, then it is more likely to be found Blu-tacked to the walls of GP surgeries, sensible advice printed onto cheap flyers advertising helpline numbers. But GP surgeries are a little like church confessionals: few of us face the issues we face in there on the outside. And so the unforgiving realities of new parenthood continue to lie submerged, unspoken, and we all perpetuate the lie that it is easy, that we can cope. But can we, can we really? Does anyone? Making three from two is inelegant maths, and having a child for the first time and expecting an easy ride is a little like moving to a new house at the foot of an active volcano in the hope that it won't blow.

Of course it will blow. It always blows.

(It might be worth pointing out that it blows for both mother *and* father. But new fathers wouldn't talk to me, perhaps desperate, for whatever private reason, to remain behind that veil of secrecy. Only new mothers opened up.)

Camilla Leveridge's entry into motherhood failed to follow the fairytale narrative, too. This bucked her own expectation, for she expected it to go smoothly. She was happily married, in her late 20s and, in her own words, 'ready'. The pregnancy went well and so, she says, 'it was a time full of hopes and dreams. We were going to be a fantastic parental unit.'

But then she gave birth, and everything came crashing abruptly down around her. 'No warning at all.'

Like many women going through the process of childbirth for the first time, the very barbarity of the procedure shocked her. What had, by nature, to happen here suddenly seemed unnatural, impossible and alien. Her labour was drawn out, and brutal. It went on for four days, four days of successive midwives clocking on, then clocking off, Camilla perpetually in *situ*, and weathering the echoing nurses' jokes of, 'Still here, love?' and tiring of it fast. She ended up going in for an emergency C-section under general anaesthetic. When she woke from it, several hours later and groggy, her son, Sonny, wasn't there. 'It was difficult not to feel a bit robbed,' she says. 'Here was this major event in my life, and I'd slept right through it.'

When her baby was finally presented to her, the instinctive connection mothers are told that they will feel the very moment they see their newborn did not occur. Its absence all too conspicuous, Camilla began to worry. She fretted. She spent 10 further days in hospital recovering, and by the time she was due to be discharged, the worry became all-out panic. She knew that something wasn't right. She may not have read very much about postnatal depression before giving birth, but she knew all too clearly that now she was in the merciless grip of it. Terrified of going home and facing these feelings alone, she alerted the nurses. The nurses told her that they weren't able to deal with such issues, and directed her instead to her GP.

The next few weeks were the worst of her life. She felt she was going mad, that she should check herself into the nearest mental institution. Fleetingly, she considered suicide; more seriously, she wondered whether she had better give the baby up for adoption. Home began to feel like a crazed environment. But when she and her husband took the baby for a walk, she did what everyone in her position invariably does: found a smile, and pretended that everything was normal. She looked tired, perhaps, but all new mothers look tired.

'Nobody in the outside world knew the depression I was feeling, the wild anxiety, or that terrible sense of loneliness,' she says. 'Only my husband. He knew. He stuck by me through everything, but he got it with both barrels, the poor man. He was left pulling his hair out for months.'

In what felt like one fell swoop, the transition from non-parent to parent gathering grave momentum, her isolation consumed her entirely. She lost her old friends, and couldn't make new ones. The worst feeling of all, she confesses, was the guilt. 'I felt so guilty that I wasn't getting the right bond with my son, that I wasn't a good mother.' It was only a matter of time until she began to resent his very existence. 'I just started to feel that he had upset my whole world.'

Her GP wrote a prescription for antidepressants, and kept writing them. If nothing else, Camilla says, the antidepressants got her up in the morning. 'They felt a little like drugs in that they gave me a buzz. And they helped me function, I suppose.'

But antidepressants merely dull the pain; they don't take it away. It was only when she was referred to Action for Children, the service provider and campaign organisation that works with over 370,000 children and families in the UK during their early years, that Camilla's situation improved.

'Action for Children helped me so much,' she says.

They effected a swift plan of action. Camilla was invited to local soft-play sessions for new mothers and their babies, where she could meet women in similar situations, and together each of them were able to step out from behind that veil of secrecy and confess to communal fears, their feelings of guilt, and their perceived inadequacies. Sharing united them, and also appeased their concerns: they all felt the same as one another; they could all be helped.

'I learned that I needed my son as much as he needed me, and as we started to play together, that bond did come.' She begins to smile. 'I can't tell you how much that meant to me, and how much things started to change after that.'

It was no quick fix, however. Camilla still struggled. If she failed to turn up to one of the sessions, a representative would call her, and even come by the house, if necessary. Camilla laughs dryly. 'They wanted to make sure that I was all right, that I was still alive. And they made me promise to turn up to the next one, and made sure I attended it.'

Sonny is five years old now, and though Camilla still admits to feelings of isolation – she describes herself as a little too strong-willed, a little too direct, and confesses that she doesn't make friends easily – she is nevertheless part of a community now. It's an effort, but a worthwhile one. 'I don't want my little boy to be lonely like me, so I'm making connections for him – and, I suppose, connections for myself as well.'

She says that being part of a group made her fully realise that she was not alone. That had been the worst thing about her experience: the utter conviction that she was all alone. 'I don't think I've spoken to a single mother who would describe parenthood as a breeze. It is a struggle, not just for me, but for everyone. Somehow, that's good to know, it's comforting – a relief. I just wish we could all recognise that, and face it.'

Emma Cartwright struggled as well. She was a young mother, and young mothers tend in many ways to have it even harder: they are pre-judged, looked down upon. Benefit-abusers. Anyone who wants to throw an arched eyebrow in the direction of any new mother would be in good company if they did so to a particularly youthful one.

Emma was 18, not single – not at that time, at least – but certainly unmarried. She had been in a relationship with her boyfriend for just a few months, and so the pregnancy was inevitably a surprise to all. She was just coming to the end of her school life, and had already signed up for a career in the army. She felt that things were nicely mapped out, ordered.

Disarray followed.

'To be clear, I never once worried whether I was going to be a good parent simply because of my age,' she is quick to point out when we speak. 'I was just worried about how I would cope emotionally, and financially, because money was tight. Those were my main worries.'

I talk to Emma on an overcast winter's day in her kitchen in Milton Keynes, where she lives. Now 25, she is happily married and has three children. A career in the armed forces may have been abruptly terminated due to her pregnancy, but she has moved on and has since revealed something of an entrepreneurial spirit. These days, she is making and selling clothes online. She might not be making very much money yet, she confesses, but she is enjoying the process enormously. The orders are coming in. 'I'm on Etsy now,' she says. Though she looks young, she appears older than her years, and is capable, and clever, and strong-willed. Her youngest child, not yet two, gurgles from her cot in the next room.

After discovering that she was pregnant for the first time, she and her new boyfriend tried to make a go of it. She left home, crossed town and moved in with him. This was unfamiliar territory for her, far from her family and friends. She had always known that she would want children, and that she would be a good mother, but motherhood was still a distant event. She had wanted solid foundations before starting a family, chiefly because she herself had been denied that. Her own mother had left the family home when Emma was just eight years old. They did keep in contact, but there were issues.

'Specifically alcohol. So my mother wasn't a particularly stable influence in my life. And, in my eyes at least, not a particularly good parent. She did try her hardest, and I think she knew, even from a very young age, that I would grow up to be a good parent one day in spite of her.' She pauses. 'I know that sounds absolutely awful, and I don't mean it to. But even when I have bad days as a mother, I still think I'm doing a better job than she did. That's important to me.'

Emma pauses a lot while we talk. She worries, aloud, that she sounds hard and unforgiving. But she doesn't. She sounds honest. She endured an upbringing that wasn't by anyone's reckoning ideal. Her father, too, was a complicated man, strict and manipulating. She no longer has a relationship with him. He had many children with many different women; Emma is one of nine. Growing up, she assumed an almost maternal role to her siblings because that was what was required of her. For this reason, she was perhaps more prepared than many other 18-year-olds for motherhood. She had just wanted to lead an independent life for a while first.

If she had considered abortion, she did so only fleetingly. At six weeks, she was rushed to hospital after she started bleeding, and found that she was terrified. 'Not for myself, but for the baby. I suppose I knew then that I was never going to get rid of her.'

But the pregnancy failed to cement the relationship with her boyfriend in ways Emma might have hoped. After giving birth, she became a stay-at-home mother, increasingly taunted by the four walls that surrounded her, and hemmed her in. They didn't have a car, and she couldn't afford the bus fare across town back to familiar turf. Her partner worked, while she dealt with a young daughter who was very demanding. 'She didn't sleep, she was attached to me consistently, she cried all the time.'

Her boyfriend weathered this seismic life change far more effectively than she did, but for one highly pertinent reason: he refused to allow fatherhood to impinge upon his lifestyle, his attitude, his entire outlook. He still socialised with friends, out several days during the week, and every weekend. Sunday mornings, Emma would have to tiptoe around the flat in order not to wake him while he slept off his hangover. 'Typical male immaturity, I suppose,' she says, shrugging sloping shoulders.

In those days, it wasn't only her child who was crying all the time. 'I was in tears every day myself. I told my boyfriend that I was lonely, that I was all alone, that I didn't have my friends around me any more. *Not my fault*, was his response. He said that it was me who wanted to have the baby, and that's true, it was, but it was still difficult not to resent him for not doing his part. And I did resent him.'

She battled on, as new parents do. One day, her mother came round and told her that she looked broken. She offered to babysit, and then, gradually, her siblings were encouraged to do so, too. Emma took them all up on their offer, readily, desperate to claw back a little personal time. 'I didn't want to go to clubs, didn't want to go drinking in pubs, nothing like that. I just wanted that connection again with the friends I'd lost. I wanted a takeaway in front of a DVD with my oldest friend. I loved my daughter very much, but I did miss evenings like that.'

There is, of course, all sorts of infrastructure available for new parents, but Emma says that she was never particularly aware of that for her first birth. If anyone had alerted her to NCT classes, she cannot remember them doing so. It's unlikely she would have been able to afford them anyway, she points out, and besides: 'I think I would have been daunted at the very thought of having to attend one.' I ask why.

Well, I suppose I'd have thought that the only women who went to those sorts of things would be thirty-something, non-working mothers who seem to have a very comfortable life. I'm not judging them, and I'm not jealous, but unfortunately you do feel, at 18, that you are just not going to have very much in common with those sorts of women. I'd have felt too self-conscious, perhaps because I had already felt so very judged by so many people.

As an aside, she explains that, when she was younger, she got tattoos. Today, she wishes she didn't have them, but there they still are, a taunting memory of her impetuous youth. The tattoos, she believes, marked her out. 'I remember, in the summer months, pushing the pram around town with my daughter in it, my new bump out on show in front...' She was by this stage married to a new man, and happily settled into contented family life. '... And the looks I got from people! Let's just say that it was very clear what they were thinking of me.'

And what were they thinking? 'That I was just another typical teenage mum, probably unmarried, probably on benefits, and almost certainly unfit for the task. But I've never been an unfit mother. I don't shout and swear at my kids, I'm respectful around them, and in my opinion at least I've always been what a good mum should be.'

If her words sound defensive, the way she delivers them is simply with the calm assurance of a mother of three, someone who has learned the lessons that come from experience. 'I've always hated the presumption that, if you are a young mother, if you don't look like the perfect stay-at-home wife, then you are obviously failing in some way; you are a drain on the system. Because that is simply not true. I wasn't failing my children at all, not then, not now.'

Like Camilla, Emma sought help from Action for Children, but did so quite accidentally. On a walk one morning – with her daughter, her bump, those tattoos on display – she came across a huddle of what looked like young mothers together in a park, along with an older pair of women who seemed, notionally at least, to be in charge. 'I thought it must be a group, or something.' She was, by this stage, in her early 20s, and more confident than she had been at 18. Confident enough to approach them, to introduce herself, and ask what was going on.

'It was a group run by Action for Children that brought young mothers together once a week in the hope that it would create a support network for them.'

Emma had found herself new friends, at last. She tells me about one of the young mothers she is now close to, someone who, like her several years previously, looked very young.

I remember asking her how old she was, and her being very reluctant to tell me that she was 19. She said that she was self-conscious about her age for the simple reason that she had a four-year-old. So the last few years had been pretty difficult for her – a new mother at 15, and all that goes along with that. But I have to tell you, she is one of the most solid people I've ever met. She has a new partner, another baby, her own home, and she keeps it immaculate. She is doing a brilliant job. But then, you know, single mums, and young mums, are doing brilliant jobs all the time. It's a shame there is still such a stigma attached to us.

The fact that Emma had a much more positive experience with her second and third child makes her lament the fact that it was all so protracted the first time around. Splitting up with her former boyfriend helped her exponentially to come fully into her own independence; falling in love with someone new, and getting married, cemented her position as someone in complete control of her life.

Oh, I feel very confident now, and it's nice to talk to younger mothers sometimes, just to tell them that they are not alone, and that it gets easier, and that there are people out there to talk to, to help you. I wish more people knew where to look, and how to get help, because first time around, especially if you are as young as I was, it is hard, you know? It's really hard.

Michelle Kennedy was a full 12 years older than Emma when she became a mother for the first time. Her pregnancy was planned, and she knew that the time was right to have a child because everything else in her life was already in place. 'I felt I had got to where I wanted to be. I had a good group of friends – although none of them had babies themselves yet – and I was married, and I was happy.'

She had done all the preparation that everybody is supposed to do: she got the crib, the cot, the pram. She attended the NCT classes, was drinking green juice each morning, and never scrimping on her five-a-day. But then the baby came, and she unravelled regardless.

When they are new, babies don't really give anything back, do they? You, the mother, could literally be anyone. I somehow never quite expected that, or appreciated it, beforehand. Also, I was all alone in the house, all day long. My husband was out at work – which, I have to say, I really, really resented, because there he was, still out in the world, and I was at home alone with a baby who just cried all the time.

Michelle began to think that perhaps she shouldn't have had a child after all, that she wasn't a natural mother, and had been foolish to ever think otherwise. The inability to breastfeed in particular frustrated her, because she'd read all the books about breastfeeding, and watched all the videos. How hard could it be?

I just felt that he didn't like me at all, my baby. I would hold him, and he wouldn't feed. He just sat there with his fists all bunched up at me. Everyone said that I had to breastfeed, that that first bit of milk, the colostrum... how important it was that Finn had the colostrum, because it acts as his first immunisation. But he wouldn't take it.

A health visitor visited:

… this woman squeezing my boob with a syringe, trying to get it out of me because Finn still wouldn't – couldn't – latch. And of course that made me feel horrendous. Nobody had ever told me I might struggle, but then why would they? They also didn't tell me that all babies lose weight in their first few weeks. So there he was, steadily losing weight, not feeding properly, because I couldn't do it, and so what else was I to think other than I was doing something, all of it, wrong?

One evening during the messy chaos of those first few weeks, Michelle, desperately tired, burst into tears. She sought out her husband's embrace, desperate for comfort, but the baby, echoing his mother, started crying too. Her husband went to Finn.

'And that was it! I just thought: *Right! First you stole my body! Then you stole my sleep! And now you've stolen my husband!*'

Colour flushes into her cheeks, and her laughter sounds hollow. 'Looking back on it now, I can't believe that was really me, that that was how I was thinking. But I'm sorry, it really was how I felt. I couldn't settle him, and Rich could.' Rich, her husband, had had children before. They were teenagers now. So his ability with his newborn child felt like blatant mockery to Michelle.

Elsewhere, the taunting at Starbucks continued. During one stroll with the pushchair, she dared step into her local branch when the baby chose the moment to burst into fresh tears. Michelle held firm. Coffee first, because caffeine, she felt, might help, if not him, then certainly her. 'But then the woman in front of me turned around, looked down at him in the pram and said to me: *Someone's getting hungry, I think*. And of course I just started crying, couldn't hold it back. I didn't know what else to say except that I just wanted my coffee!'

There is more laughter now. 'It was a stupid, selfish reaction, I know, but I just wanted my five minutes before I started my walk again, before I devoted myself entirely to him again. And so that was a particularly low moment.'

More were to follow. She developed mastitis; her ongoing lack of sleep left her half-mad. She began hallucinating. She visited her doctor to request tablets to help dry up her breastmilk, because she became convinced that it might be poisoning him. The doctor refused to issue her the prescription, but instead asked her to fill out a questionnaire about whether or not she was feeling suicidal.

A sleep trainer was employed, the kind of mythical, wart-nosed nanny that most people believe only exist in Hollywood films. It seems they exist in real life, too. This one, albeit minus the wart, came into Michelle's house, bringing her stern expression and broad hips with her, and announced that the problem was not her baby boy, but her, Michelle.

'She told me that I hadn't got him into any routine yet, that he owned me, that I did everything he wanted me to. But *that's what you're meant to do, aren't you?!* I asked back.'

The sleep trainer initiated a routine, to which Michelle firmly adhered. After a few long and desperate days, her boy did indeed start to sleep more, and so, in merciful tandem, did she. Gradually, her situation alleviated, but still she was away from work, from colleagues and friends, and her daily interaction with others remained severely restricted: occasional visits from her in-laws; an over-reliance upon her mother.

'It's fascinating just how much of your life changes,' she notes. 'I've been working since I was 15, and I have made a lot of sacrifices along the way to get ahead in my career. But when the baby came along, all that was put on hold.' But not, she points out, for Rich, her husband. For him, as with so many men, life carried on much as before. 'He would come home from work and tell me about a deal he was working on, and all I could tell him in return was that Finn had done three poos...'

Something had to give, to change. One can only discuss shit so many times, after all. Though she might have been more at home in NCT groups, they had appealed as much to her as they had to Emma Cartwright. Michelle says that she often feels socially awkward, that she is not 'everybody's cup of tea.' When she is nervous, she suggests, 'I talk a lot, too quickly, I can be a bit too much for some people. So I struggled to connect with anyone in those classes.'

Post-birth, there was no immediate equivalent, either. Those soft-play cafés don't really apply until a baby is at least three months old, which leaves, says Michelle, 'Ninety full days in which the parent is all by themselves, alone and often tortured.'

Why was it so difficult, she wondered, to meet like-minded new mothers, when the sheer numbers involved suggest that like-minded mothers surrounded her?

'Oh, I really struggled to establish a new social group, and I really did try. I remember bumping into one girl one day, also a new mum, and I asked her for her number. She said to me: *You know what? I'm not going to take your number because I have a lot of friends already, and I don't want to let you down.'* As Michelle recounts this episode, she crosses her legs and hugs her arms. 'The most crushingly mortifying moment of my life!'

So she did something drastic but, she felt, necessary. Two years after returning to work following her maternity leave, she left her position at Badoo, the dating app, to create another one – this one for new mothers who felt, as she had once, a desperate craving for company. Peanut, as the app is called, connects individuals with people at the same stage as they are, whether on maternity leave or back working full- or part-time. Young mothers can meet young mothers, older ones older ones. Separating the supermums from all the ordinary versions, and the high achievers from the stay-at-homes, the user can, in just three swift swipes, arrange to meet with someone with whom the app believes they will connect on a tangible level.

'I know a lot of people are of the belief that technology just makes people even more lonely,' she concedes, 'but my response to that is: define lonely. When you are doing a night feed at 2 a.m., and you are suddenly able to find a new mum doing exactly the same thing online, does that make you feel lonelier, or does it make you feel better? I can tell you it would have made me feel *much* better.'

Peanut, she says, is not about keeping people apart, but about using the technology around us – social media, the way we organise our lives today – for good, to help connect people to other people. 'I was a lonely new mother when I didn't need to be. Now, I hope, new mothers will be able to avoid what I, and so many others, went through. And that has to be a good thing, right?'

Directory

Action for Children

www.actionforchildren.org.uk/

01923 361 500

Peanut

https://www.peanut-app.io/

EIGHT

Technical support

When looking for scapegoats, for potential reasons why we are all feeling increasingly separated from one another, more and more of us point towards technology as the overriding reason. If we weren't all so focused upon our phones all the time, we might still be focused upon those around us. In the American psychology writer Jean M. Twenge's 2017 book, *iGen*, which laboured under the unwieldy subheading: *Why Today's Super-Connected Kids Are Growing Up Less Rebellious, More Tolerant, Less Happy – And Completely Unprepared for Adulthood – and What That Means for the Rest of Us,*[9] she suggests that so-called 'iGen' teens – those born in 1995 or later, who grew up with mobile phones, had Instagram pages before they started high school, and do not remember a time before the internet – spend less time at parties than any previous generation.

Asking why parties, once the defining event for teenagers everywhere, have become less popular, one iGenner tells her: 'Now we have Netflix – you can watch series non-stop. [Also] there's so many things to do on the web.'

Television appeals more than real life does. For those who do still want to socialise, they do so via Snapchat, connected but alone, each adrift in their rooms, nestled into their childhood duvets, the lights on low; the very picture of a very twenty-first-century kind of hermit.

Technology undeniably robs us of human contact, but the truth is that tech is only as culpable as the people who drive it. Much of today's technology is focused around keeping us all connected, all of the time. If, subsequently, we still fail to make those connections we foster online into real-life relationships, who, ultimately, is to blame? Did the telephone, when it became so intrinsic a part of everybody's lives during the twentieth century, receive quite as much flak as its smartphone counterpart does today?

Technology, argues Karen Dolva, a woman who works in the tech sector but does so with the explicit aim of improving lives and our sense of connectedness, is simply what we make it to be. A 28-year-old Norwegian who created a start-up to help those who are socially isolated to reconnect with the wider world around them, she believes that the way we have been using so much of modern technology is, simply, wrong. We need to realign.

'Until now, we've been focused on improving our efficiency and making us faster and faster, while our conversations are supposed to be shortened down instead of being prolonged,' Dolva says.

I think that is the completely wrong way of looking at it. But this isn't technology's fault; it's the people who are making the technology, and the way we are then using it. As long as we remember that *we* are still in control of it, then why shouldn't it help make all areas of our life easier for everyone, to help people go to places that they can't, or to be with their families more?

Her tech company, No Isolation, was founded in Norway in October 2015 with just a single purpose in mind: to reduce involuntary social isolation. The initial idea was to direct their efforts towards the older generation, which, as we have seen, experiences the most isolation, and most sharply. But, Dolva says, they soon realised that there were lots of initiatives – technological and otherwise – for that demographic already.

'And so we chose to focus on children, on children with long-term health conditions, and those that have to spend a lot of time at home or in hospital because of it. Because, really, what happens to these children when they get sick?'

Children's attention spans are short. So when a child is absent from school, and remains so for a period of time, they quickly lose their entire connection to the world outside their immediate environment. 'It is difficult,' says Dolva, 'for someone to remember someone else who is not there anymore, even more so if you happen to be 8, 12, or even 14. It's impossible to keep fully in touch with someone if you don't constantly meet up with them, and interact with them. In other words, the second that child is taken out of their sight, they lose everything. In a couple of weeks,' she suggests, 'it is almost like their peers have forgotten they ever existed.'

Some may take issue with Dolva's rather pessimistic claims – are children really quite so wilfully forgetful? – but it was with this certainty in mind that her company went to work, creating something that could represent the absent child in its stead. Called the AV1, it's that most futuristic of all our futuristic obsessions: a robot, a small, pillowy-looking thing made of tactile plastic, and dyed the colour of marshmallows. It resembles something Pixar might have dreamt up on a wet Thursday afternoon with a view to transforming it into a franchise whose likeness is then sold at toy shops in time for Christmas. It looks like it requires an *awful lot* of batteries.

But the AV1 is more than cute. It is the world's first telepresence robot specifically designed for children and young adults with long-term illnesses. By sending it to school, the child at home (or in hospital) can continue to participate in class, and maintain contact with their school friends. Their school friends then need not ever forget they existed.

The child controls it through an app on their tablet to act as their eyes and ears, even their voice. They can signal that they want to speak up by instructing a light on its head to blink. They can turn it 360° in order to see all around them; they can talk to their classmates, or direct a question to the teacher. There is even a function that allows them to whisper to friends outside of adult earshot. Whenever they don't want to participate, they can simply turn on a blue light at the top of its head.

Few, surely, could argue that this isn't an example of technology making the world a better place for all who live in it.

'It's very adaptable,' says Dolva, 'and the child's diagnosis is irrelevant. Doctors tend to tell sick children that they need to rest, and of course they do. But they also need to talk, to interact, to communicate with people.'

In trials undertaken to date, it has proved very successful. Children adapt to the avatar quickly, the novelty its main selling point. It's fun, and children like fun. It is the adults that need persuading. 'The teachers, we sometimes have to explain it to more fully,' Dolva says. 'But for computer-literate kids, avatars are very easy to grasp. They get it right away.'

There are plans to make the AV1 available worldwide, initially to children, but later to other age groups as well. Right now, there are 220 representing young people across Scandinavia and Britain. One of them has found its way to the north-east of England, just off the A1, in Durham, in a small town called Newton Hall. It belongs to a young woman by the name of Jade Gadd.

When she was 14 years old, Jade Gadd was practising tae kwon do at her family's Wabi-Sabi Academy in Durham. Wabi-Sabi is a Japanese worldview centred on the acceptance of transience and imperfection. In this case, in England's north-east, it translated into a centre for health, vitality and mindfulness, with its own connected tearoom. Jade was good at tae kwon do, good enough to be a part-time trainer to other children.

'Every day I was doing physical training to try to make myself stronger,' she tells me. 'But then one day, my shoulder dislocated. And that was it, pretty much.'

Like her mother, her aunt, at least one cousin, her grandfather and great grandmother, Jade suffers from hypermobile Ehlers-Danlos syndromes (EDS), a rare hereditary condition that causes different systems of the body to shut down without warning. In many ways, Jade knew this was coming. What she couldn't have anticipated was the severity of her own case. While her mother found it suspiciously easy to click all 10 toes, and while her grandmother could give birth at terrific speed due to easily dislocated hips – one of the more memorable family stories is of how Grandma was peeling potatoes one afternoon when she stopped suddenly to go to the toilet; she delivered the baby, and then came back downstairs to resume her task at the sink – Jade's was more pronounced. Pertinently, it was far worse. Her joints became so loose, her blood pressure falling so low, that intermittently she could, and indeed did, lose her sight, her hearing, her speech. She found it increasingly difficult to move, and when she did, there was much pain. Her spine no longer felt fit for purpose.

'The way it works with a lot of people is that it doesn't really show up properly until people go through some kind of trauma,' Jade, now 18, says. For her, that trauma was puberty. 'When I turned 13, things started to get really loose really quickly. I dislocated a lot, and after that – well, after that, everything got progressively worse.'

For the next four years, Jade was in and out of hospital. When back at home, she was often confined to bed. Today, a typical day is one of pain. It emanates from her spine and spreads outwards, like wildfire.

'To be honest with you, I'm probably going through more pain than I strictly should be,' she says. 'But that's only because I said no to the medication.' She explains that she got sick of feeling like a zombie, and wanted instead to experience life, 'not just as a weird blur that went on around me, but as it really is. So I stopped with all the pills. I thought to myself: if this is what I need to go through in order to experience the world, then this is what I need to do.'

Jade also has Asperger's, which affects the way she processes the sensory world around her. Add this to the EDS, and life can seem cruelly complicated. She is, unambiguously, severely afflicted. But it is a curious, and humbling, experience talking to Jade. At 18, she has endured more pain and suffering than many of us will in a lifetime. The sheer ignominy of having a rare disease so very few people have ever heard of would, you'd think, be draining enough, but her life force remains a palpable one. She is ringingly bright, clever and funny. She smiles a lot when, by rights, she should be doing anything but.

School quickly fell by the wayside. By the time she was consigned to a wheelchair, she had already suffered at the hands of bullies, and so had withdrawn herself accordingly. When the bullying continued online, this to her was simply another cross to bear. She was fast losing count of all the many crosses she bore.

In 2016, there came at least the possibility of some good news when she became the eager recipient of an AV1. She had been in hospital for a long time by this point, and had been reliant upon the tutor that visited the wards most weekday mornings. By the time she returned home, she was no longer either physically or mentally prepared for the rigours of a classroom. And so she sent out the robot on her behalf.

At first, she says, she loved it. 'It was a novelty. And it was nice to be out in the world again, to see things outside my house. I've been stuck in my bedroom for quite a while, so just to be able to see different things, the faces of my friends at school, even some faces I'd never seen before, was definitely a good thing. Yes,' she says, nodding, 'it was just so lovely to see so many different faces.'

Her head of sixth form was initially bemused by the avatar, and other teachers later reported to her that they similarly found it, 'a bit weird.'

'One teacher said it was like talking to a toy that was possessed by me.'

School friends, however, were more accepting. Those who had never been her friends in the first place simply gave it, and by association her, the wide berth they'd always given her. 'I've not been the best at making friends, so it's difficult to say whether they were ignoring me any more than they would have done normally,' she says, laughing. 'But, you know, it got me back into the classroom again, and learning again, amongst others. I liked that.'

It also allowed her to continue to struggle in private. She says she is glad that the avatar doesn't have a screen, and that she cannot be seen on it, because, 'I don't want to have to hold my head up and look normal, pretending that my spine doesn't hurt for a lot of the time, because it does. So it's nice just to be able to lie back in bed if I have to.'

On better days, friends have taken her 'out' with them, showing her the town, the park, or wherever they happened to wander. Recently, she has joined a Dungeons & Dragons group, and is able to take part in games alongside these friends. 'So I get to kill dragons with the robot, which I imagine is something a lot of people in Dungeons & Dragons would love to be able to say!'

The AV1 is currently helping her study for her A-levels, after which she is considering university. 'The only limit I see with the robot is the limit on my own imagination. As long as the internet connection is there, I can go pretty much anywhere with this. Okay, maybe not the moon, but *most* places.'

By *most places*, she means Comic-Con, the convention for comic fans. 'Oh, I'd love it if one day my friends took me – or it, the robot – to a Comic-Con.' She thinks that in such an environment, a gadget like the AV1 would likely go down very well indeed. She might be more readily embraced there than she is elsewhere.

In almost every area of her necessarily compartmentalised life, Jade Gadd sees only the positive. Of the ongoing cyber bullying she is having to endure, she simply shrugs and says: 'That's just an example of bad technology, I suppose. But then technology is only as good as we allow it to be through our own actions, wouldn't you say?' And as the robot's very existence proves, she adds, 'technology can also be good, it can be amazing. I couldn't have done everything I've managed to do without this robot, and without the technology that powers it. I'm very grateful for it.'

She tells me that she has been exposed to a lot of 'awesome people' lately, and the way in which she says that word – *awesome* – suggests that it is a relatively new word to her, and that she likes it. 'And so I've decided that I want to become an awesome person myself. I don't know exactly what it is I'm going to do with my life, but whatever it is, I want to be the kind of person that, when others talk about me, they go: *Oh yeah, she's an awesome person!*'

What Jade doesn't realise yet is that she already *is*.

Directory

No Isolation
https://www.noisolation.com/uk/

Campaign to End Loneliness
https://www.campaigntoendloneliness.org

NINE

University challenged

Anna Warren arrived at university, where she would be studying politics, in a state of some excitement. 'I don't get very excited about many things,' she deadpans, 'but I was definitely excited to be here. These years are supposed to be the best years of your life, right?'

At university, she was a full hour and a half from home, and this was good. It meant independence! Here, she could throw herself into a brand-new life. The first few days were a whirl.

Most people, I suppose, were just like me: they didn't know anybody else, either. So everybody was getting lots of invitations – to bars, to parties. On campus, there was like an open house policy, everyone in and out of everyone else's flats. It was fun, but somehow I found that the people I met on my first few days there, I almost never saw again. I'm not really sure why, but nobody seemed to remember anybody's name, there didn't seem to be any email exchanges, or phone numbers. I guess it was too casual for that. I'd been hoping to make friends, but it didn't really turn out that way.

Anna moved into a flatshare, along with five others. Only one of her flatmates was on the same course as her, and each was busy with their own life. They all got along well enough, but there was no bonding, no cementing of lasting friendships late into the night. Like most flatmates, she supposed, they would congregate over breakfast or, late in the evening, around the microwave, but otherwise they all remained in their own individual bubbles; many rarely even emerged from their respective rooms. Fair enough, Anna thought. Just because people lived together didn't mean they had to become the best of friends. This wasn't *Friends*. Besides, she was lucky, ish: they could all have hated one another, and that did not seem to be the case here.

But still, she craved lasting company, new relationships. She sought out social groups more associated to her studies. Future political types were convivial sorts, right? On campus, she found several clubs and societies, many revolving around activities like sport, though some were political. Eventually, she joined the debating society. Quickly, she regretted it.

'It turned out not to be the best place to make friends, really. Most of the people who attended just ended up arguing with one another.' She smiles. 'I suppose that's the whole point of debating...'

She hoped she might forge close bonds with those in her lectures. If she were ever to meet like-minded individuals, then surely it would be in the classroom, fellow students studying the same thing as she was. But in lecture halls, unlike in school classrooms, students can sit wherever they like. Many have arrived from different lecture halls, at different times, and so Anna found it difficult to sit next to the same person on consecutive days. At the end of each class, the students quickly drifted out, eyes to their phones, headphones in, stalking off to who knows where, always in a rush.

'It was then that I started to realise just how difficult it was going to be to properly socialise at university, and I'm not sure I really expected that,' she says.

I suppose I'm generally quite an independent person, so I was fine being alone, but it is difficult when you see your flatmates getting together to do something, but not inviting you. Why not me? That was the hardest part, I think: the sense of being left out, left behind. Because, you know, I wanted to be included. I wanted to go to the parties they were going to; I wanted to be social. Instead, I ended up in my room with a pizza. I ate a lot of pizza alone in my room that first term.

The situation persisted, and then it became the norm. Anna was alone. Quite why she was failing to make new friends in a place that seemed to be swarming with people who had become just that – new friends – wasn't clear. 'All I knew was that other people appeared to be managing it, but not me.'

After several weeks, she began to tentatively look into what people in her situation do if they want to alleviate it. She learned that there was somewhere on campus that offered assistance. 'There is this whole building where they have counsellors you can go to speak to, but to be honest, I felt very strange and awkward even considering doing something like that. I mean, can you imagine me going up to the reception and announcing myself, then sitting there waiting to talk to someone I'd never met before about how lonely I was?'

And as for the student bar: 'People who go to the student bar tend to go in twos and threes. Those on their own stand out. I didn't really want to stand out.'

Options exhausted, Anna came to deal with her growing loneliness the way many university students ultimately do: in private, and in secret. She confessed to hardly anyone back home how she was feeling, and certainly not her parents. Instead, she knuckled down to focus on her course, and completed all the reading she was required to do, and more. She was aware of her tutor on the periphery, someone whom the university literature had suggested she might be able to call upon, if the situation arose, but there was a problem here, too. 'The tutor I'd been assigned to, I'm not taught by, so I don't know him. I've met him once, I think. So I would feel very weird talking to him, this complete stranger, about such a personal issue.'

She tried to make the best of the situation, and to better appreciate it. She was young, just 18, her first time away from home. Many of those around her had taken gap years, and were a full year older. So of course she was going to feel younger than them, and generally less experienced. Perhaps she would catch up in time? Perhaps things would be better the following term, or if not then, in her second year?

But how long was Anna supposed to look forward? When would she start feeling more settled, happier, in her new situation? When I spoke to her, she was just coming to the end of her first term, and change was already afoot. Several of her flatmates had begun to pair off and were keen to move on, making her believe that they had connected with one another after all, while she hadn't.

'And so I suppose I'm still struggling with it all,' she told me.

I've no intention of leaving the course, nothing like that. It's not that bad yet, and I hope I don't end up feeling that way over time. I just know that I'm going to have to start to learn to be a bit more resourceful, and independent. I accept that; it's what you have to do in life. But I can't help but wish it was all just a little bit easier, not just for me but for others. I can't be the only one struggling to adapt to all this, can I? That's what I keep telling myself, anyway.

The outside perception of university life runs in marked contrast to Anna's current experience of it. The very notion of further education remains appealing in so many ways. University represents the beginning of us in adult life, these institutions where we at last get to expand our universe, uncover our potential, develop our interests, our very belief systems. They offer us a chance of true independence, of being able to stand on our own two feet, a state many of us might have been waiting impatiently to begin for some considerable time. It's a period when we get to challenge our assumptions and prejudices, where we are permitted to step into who we really are, who we might be, and what we might go on to become. Also, the bar sells cheap beer.

But, it seems, the actual reality – or perhaps the *new* reality – of university life is not quite as rose-tinted. Everyone I spoke to returned to the same theme, that universities are run now as big businesses, for profit. Anonymous monoliths, largely impervious to individual needs. Those who don't keep up don't keep up. Debt, the spectre of, now plays a major part, its shadow encroaching on the very first day, then lengthening over time by stealth.

I wanted to speak to someone from within its hierarchy to help give me an accurate insight from their perspective. Is it really as bleak as Anna suggests, really quite as hard to fit in, to acclimatise? Is such a rude culture shock unavoidable, and the chances of eventually settling perpetually problematical?

I struggled. Finding available spokespeople proved an unexpectedly difficult task. Spokespeople, I learned, don't really exist in this area, at least not willing ones. I hit many dead ends, and came up against much reluctance. My emails became an annoyance, and were ultimately ignored; my phone calls screened. Of the two dozen or more university receptionists I spoke to, more than one responded with a 'Who?' when I asked to speak to a student union representative, or someone I could talk to about the student experience. Even those campuses that boasted impressive websites where a sense of community and wellbeing was extolled, failed to offer up anyone prepared to talk.

'I don't know why you were put through to me,' one young man said when we spoke. 'See, I'm not really sure who runs our website, but it's not me.'

I explained what I wanted to talk about, and that I was hoping to highlight the efforts extended to help make student life more amenable to all, effectively to highlight their hard work. He responded glumly, by saying that he didn't know what to tell me. 'I'll ask around, and get back to you.'

He never got back to me.

But eventually I did find someone to talk to. Perhaps pertinently, it was someone who had recently retired from the profession, and was therefore, in a sense, off the hook, answerable to no one any longer. Dr Ron Roberts was a senior lecturer and chartered psychologist who had spent over 20 years researching the mental health of students within our university system. The results he uncovered proved not for the faint of heart. So stark were his findings that those for whom he undertook the research in the first place – the university body itself – developed deaf ears, and ultimately suggested he cease his research.

'The research showed that suicide within university students was on the rise,' Dr Roberts tells me, 'but they didn't want to hear about suicide statistics.'

Dr Roberts had been trying to help create, and sustain, a better climate. In a paper he co-authored shortly before his retirement, he wrote of the growing sense of isolation students feel today, and how this might be avoided. 'Encouraging participation in societies and activities, and offering mentoring schemes provided by other students or tutors, could help alleviate students' feelings of loneliness, and therefore decrease the likelihood of them developing mental health problems over time.'

But, time and again, his advice was summarily glossed over, ignored, dismissed.

When I talk to him about his work, Dr Roberts doesn't hold back. He sounds exhausted, and exasperated, frequently angry. But then his prognosis is almost entirely bleak, and the picture he paints for me, and indeed for anyone considering further learning, is not an attractive one.

What we found was that there was a very high incidence rate amongst university students developing eating disorders, alcohol problems – the whole range, really. There were many mental health issues as a result, and our findings were unambiguous: universities don't do enough to help their students. They need to be doing much more, clearly. The management companies that run universities today like to suggest that they are putting the student experience at the very centre of education, but I'm sorry, that is a barefaced lie. They just want to attain high student satisfaction scores but actually do precious little to improve the experience at all.

He says that when he was asked to stop working on his research, it was with the foolish hope that by ignoring the growing problem, the growing problem would simply go away. It didn't.

'It got worse, inevitably. An increasing number of students drop out as a result of student debt.' And those who stay face ongoing financial anxiety. Not all students can, or want to, do bar work, and so more and more, Dr Roberts found, were turning to sex work to help fund their studies: webcam transactions, stripping, prostitution. This brought with it a whole raft of new and associated complications. A further 10 per cent of university students, meanwhile, are parents, a factor that only adds to their educational burdens.

If such problems are endemic to university life, it is likely because many people arrive at their place of further education with a number of psychological issues in place, issues that were not successfully treated at the time they first arose, in earlier life – at school, at home. They simmer to the surface on campus, largely due to these added pressures, and universities are then blamed for not dealing with them accordingly. A hostile environment here can only worsen the problem. All the more reason, Dr Roberts insists, for working hard to make the whole environment as friendly and welcoming as possible.

> There are many reasons why university can be so problematical for so many. Partly it's because students have just left home, a familiar environment for a completely new city, often in a distant part of the country. They are now in a new and unfamiliar place where they have to quickly form new social ties, find somewhere to live, and generate enough money to sustain themselves. Then they've got their courses to focus on. Loneliness does set in, but as our research has found, the loneliness they feel at the beginning of their studies often persists throughout their entire time there. And because we have so many more people in higher education these days [the number of university students in the UK has doubled since the early 1990s], it of course becomes a bigger and bigger issue.

Universities do make some effort, at least initially, he concedes, but these are too transient. It takes more to make a new student feel at home than simply introducing them to the bar, and then directing them to the nearest counselling centre in the event they might at some point require it.

These welcoming initiatives last for one week, perhaps two, but then that's it, they disappear, and the student is on their own. That's crazy when you consider that the challenges the students face are very likely to be continuous, and ongoing. So where are the mentoring schemes, the second- and third-year students looking out for, and helping, the new entrants to settle in?

He is also at pains to point out that it is not only students that suffer in modern universities. The staff, too, face more stress.

The corporate takeover of higher education in the UK today has completely altered the landscape for further education. The staff are under more pressure than ever. There is massively increased bureaucracy, which means that staff have less time to spend with their students. There is a lot of bullying of staff from management, and so no wonder it's an unfriendly environment because, frankly, teachers are dealing with an absurd level of overload. The result? Everybody suffers.

Dr Roberts reiterates that there are potential solutions, and ones that should be easy enough to implement if only all concerned could be bothered. There should be more social events, more reaching out, not merely from staff but from the students themselves.

Several months after speaking to Dr Roberts, I locate someone within the student union body itself willing to talk to me. He asks to remain anonymous, explaining that universities tend to be very conscious of their media image, especially if that image might tip towards the unflattering. Being honest with me here, on the page, will likely do his career few favours. So no names.

After we speak, however, I am left with the conviction that he is representative of a student union body in general that works incredibly hard to help its students, and whose presence on and around campus isn't actually as faceless and anonymous as can sometimes appear. Yes, they are struggling to connect, but then this is an enormous issue for which there is no easy fix. Critics are everywhere.

'It's a difficult business, running universities,' he tells me, 'and so even when effort is expended, not everybody's going to be happy. So if you have found it difficult finding people prepared to talk to you, I'm not surprised. It's a subject people are nervous to discuss openly because of its complexity.'

He explains that every university will have its own student welfare counselling service, places where students are actively encouraged to turn up to whenever they might be in need of assistance. They are well advertised, amply staffed. 'Though we can't make them go, of course,' he points out.

In theory, these places should be as overrun as the average GP waiting room, but they're not. Many campuses around the country are working hard to correct this. There is a duty of care here, perhaps now more than ever given that universities charge fees, taking an average of £9000 per year from every student. For every student that drops out, the university itself loses money. And that's no way to run a business.

'This isn't to suggest that every student now has a pound sign above their heads,' the spokesperson says, 'but each financial director will nevertheless look at it like that. Ultimately, we shouldn't be losing students; we should be looking at why they drop out in the first place, and then try to foster a better sense of belonging for them, initiatives that will help each student feel part of something bigger and not merely on a conveyor belt that simply gets them their degree before spitting them out into the world.'

Nevertheless, the universities' main role remains an academic one. These are places of higher learning, and as such have their own targets to reach. So while they will indeed signpost places where students can go to get support outside of the classroom, it is the classroom itself that must continue to concern them most. Pastoral care lies elsewhere.

'Cost is a driving factor in universities,' he says, 'and so funding will always be directed towards the teaching itself. But I would like to underline that there is effort being made here by many people to make the experience of university life beneficial to everyone. We want every student to have a positive experience.'

In the meantime, then, students are increasingly helping one another, and looking out for one another more – if not always face-to-face, then at least online, where compassion comes easier. In the continued absence of wholly successful management-led initiatives, the students are finding each other on forums. They need to. Because, as Anna Warren suggests, she's not the only one struggling.

Chelsea Sowden is in her first year of university, studying animation. She too has had a hard time fitting in, but her experiences have been compounded by health issues: she has chronic fatigue and fibromyalgia. These twin conditions – chronic fatigue leaves her exhausted, and fibromyalgia in a lot of pain – rendered her school years, in her words, 'pretty horrific'. She struggled through her GCSEs and A-levels, but convinced herself that university might constitute a fresh start. Things might get better, at last. She'd certainly earned her place there.

'But it was still difficult,' she admits. 'A lot of the initial social activities were centred around pubs and alcohol, which isn't always great for meeting new people – or not for me, at least. I would try to go out with everyone, but then I would lose them, and that would be the end of that.'

When her fibromyalgia flares up, the pain can be crippling. Sometimes, she has to walk with crutches. She thought she might have better luck making new friends at social events specifically directed towards disabled students. 'I knew I couldn't be the only person with a disability there, but I couldn't find any events, no notices, nothing like that.'

Living in halls, she had her own room in a flat with seven others. 'But they pretty much kept themselves to themselves. Some had boyfriends or girlfriends, and three of the girls seemed to get very close very quickly, and then just existed within their own little clique.'

Like Anna Warren, she did manage to make some friends on her course, but none of the friendships ran particularly deep. 'I kept thinking to myself: why am I struggling? You know, here I am turning up to all the society events, but I get there on my own, and I leave on my own. It's all been pretty depressing, really.'

At another university, an hour north of Chelsea Sowden's, Sophie Jones is in her fourth and final year of her studies, currently pursuing her Masters in Public Health. She tells me that her first two years of university life were among the worst experiences she has had. 'I almost dropped out multiple times, simply because I couldn't hack it. I found making friends just so hard. I struggled so much.'

But things did improve for her over time, or rather she worked hard to improve her situation. She did make friends, eventually, after two long years. She puts it down to luck, but there was also an awful lot of sheer dogged persistence. 'Oh, definitely. I couldn't have got to where I am today – happy, contented, with friends – without having gone through that awful loneliness period at the beginning. At first, I didn't particularly get on with my flatmates, and I suppose I just didn't have the sufficient social skills, or the drive. And you need both if you are going to survive in an environment like this.'

Sophie identifies herself as a very anxious person, particularly in an academic setting. Like so many people, she had arrived at university with psychological issues that had first developed at school. She had been bullied a lot, largely she believes because of her height. 'I'm ridiculously short, 4'9". I looked different, and that was enough for people to make fun of me. Simple as that.'

Though the bullying stopped at university, she found that her new peer group still searched for instantly visible commonalities to help them bond, commonalities they did not find in her. She made no friends during her first year, and precious few in her second.

'I convinced myself that absolutely nobody wanted to talk to me, so I just kept thinking to myself: why am I even here? Why am I even bothering?'

Like many other students in her situation, she wasn't keen on the on-campus counselling options.

I suppose that was simply because I already knew what my issues were: anxiety around people. And I knew what I had to do to get over that: just get out there and talk to those people! Counselling just strikes me as a lot of back-and-forth talking, and I didn't need that. These were steps I had to take by myself, and, you know, eventually I did. You can talk to a counsellor until you are blue in the face, but a counsellor is never going to come with you on a night out and actually make friends for you, are they? That's something you've got to do by yourself.

But Sophie, like Chelsea, did reach out for help somewhere. Both of them turned online, to a website called The Student Room, a peer-platform that helps young people make informed life choices, alongside answering the usual growing-up questions that we all face; Mumsnet for the mostly childfree. Those who found it difficult to talk openly about their issues found they had few such problems interacting on The Student Room's many forums that, between them, covered every issue, every quibble, and most eventualities. Those that focus on depression and loneliness receive particularly high traffic.

Chelsea started to post anonymously, and quickly found friends. 'And I can't tell you how much it has helped me,' she says. 'Everyone is very understanding on there, and they can all relate. It draws people like me in, and definitely makes us feel less alone.'

Chelsea now volunteers at The Student Room herself, giving advice as she had once received it. Her sense of isolation, she says, has now largely lifted as a consequence. Her relief is evident.

I feel very close to a lot of my online friends now, but it does worry me in one sense. I seem to be able to make friends online really easily but I still have difficulty doing so in real life. Why? I suppose I feel I can say whatever I want online without having the same consequences of doing so in person. I can be more honest. If somebody responds badly, I just block them. I can't do that in real life. Shame, really!

The Student Room was set up in 2001 in direct response to the need for advice on university applications alongside more general life-around-learning questions. It was an instant hit, and now receives seven million page views a month. The reason it works, says Hannah Morrish, who works in its community team, is because it focuses on students helping students, no outside interference.

'There is only so much a lecturer or teacher, or even a parent, can say,' Hannah says.

Advice like this really has to come from someone in a similar situation, someone who has lived through it and come out the other side. And we're not just here to help combat the stresses of university life, by the way; we are here to support people on their journey throughout their lives, helping them to make informed decisions relating to their relationships, their mental health, their education, career choices, everything.

Hannah echoes Dr Roberts' assertion that university life is almost invariably a hotbed of psychological issues that, having long festered, now blossom.

Universities are definitely picking up on a lot of the trauma that young people have already carried throughout their education – the pressures of doing well in exams, showcasing a perfect life on social media, applying for the most prestigious universities, family responsibilities and navigating complex friendships and romantic relationships. All this takes a toll. When students then leave for university, they leave their comfort zone, their security blanket and all the usual ways of fulfilling their emotional and physical needs. This can then trigger all the pressure and stress that's built up over time, fuelling anxiety and self-esteem issues. University students really do need help in picking up the pieces when their mental health begins to come crashing down. It's a huge lifestyle change, and not one that everyone naturally flourishes in from the beginning.

For Sophie Jones, struggling with intermittent loneliness through four long years of university has given her the strength and resilience to face the rest of what life will throw her way. The experience, often unpleasant, has helped her raise her game. She has mettle now.

I suppose it's taught me how to cope, even when things get really difficult. And it's helped me learn how to open up to people, and to be more confident. I won't lie to you, it was a really big challenge, but then that's what life is all about: one big challenge after another. At least I now feel ready for them.

Directory

The Student Room

https://www.thestudentroom.co.uk/

Nightline Association

https://www.nightline.ac.uk/

TEN

Blind man's bluff

The daily pressure to conform to what can sometimes seem like a cookie-cutter society, in which we accept only those who are, to extend the metaphor, the same shape, and boast the same ingredients as us, is another reason why many of us might struggle with a pervading sense of social isolation in life. If we don't measure up on Instagram, we're in trouble. Or if we don't have enough likes on Facebook; if our place of work is full of sociopaths; if we are ostracised at the school gates, the playground, the university campus. In a world of seven billion souls, where every one of us is different and yet every one of us must in some way conform, a significant proportion might simply prefer to conceal our differences in order to better blend in with the highly demanding requirements of the otherwise nebulous crowd.

But not everyone can blend in quite so successfully. One sector that can, and does, struggle more than most is the disabled. Those who are not as able-bodied as everybody else, who have mental or physical challenges, will stick out more. This in itself is not a problem: the problem is *everybody else*, because society isn't always particularly good at accommodating what society might view, cruelly, carelessly, and without basis, *anomalies*.

Sense is the disability charity that was started 60 years ago for families whose children were suffering with rubella syndrome, a condition that affects sight and hearing. The charity launched with the aim of developing knowledge and expertise in order to help those affected and, later in life, assisting with accommodation and educational provision. Their remit has extended over the decades into supporting people with complex communication needs, to help them remain connected and, more importantly still, *valued*. It can often be difficult for society to look beyond someone's impairment, to seek what we might have in common when what we don't is so immediately recognisable. Many blind people, for example, will say they view their cane, or guide dog, as something that may well facilitate their everyday life but that also hinders them dramatically, stigmatising them as it does in the eyes of everybody else. To even consider picking up a cane, for some, is like drinking from the poisoned chalice, and accepting an unavoidable fate: pity, scorn, exclusion.

Mark Baxter is a 36-year-old who works for the charity as a support team administrator. Mark has a degenerative eye condition called retinitis pigmentosa (RP), a hereditary condition which struck shortly before his 10th birthday. Today, he sees the world only at the end of a very long tunnel. His peripheral vision is mostly gone. Night blindness has become an issue.

'I did my very best not to let it stop me from living my life,' Mark tells me, brightly. At school, for example, he played rugby for as long as he could. He pursued an active social life, and went out with friends at night because, 'why wouldn't I?' He considers himself lucky. 'RP can develop very quickly. Mine had a slower progression.'

He has been registered blind since 2014. What he can see of the world now is filtered through a milky mucus. Initially, I had been communicating with him via text. Text messages have become for him problematical but not yet impossible. Because he can no longer make out black words on a white background – the white bleaches, then saturates, everything – he has an app on his phone that switches black-on-white to white-on-black. 'It helps,' he says. At other times, he uses a magnifier.

Mark has been using a cane to get about for several years now. He refuses to be restricted by his impairment, despite the obstacles, both metaphorical and literal, in his path. 'I've been hit by cars on more than one occasion,' he says. 'Cracked six ribs last time.' Now he smiles. 'But, you know, it makes me stronger, wiser. I don't plan to be on the bonnet of a car again any time soon.'

But his main day-to-day challenges, he explains, concern not the blindness itself so much as the attitude of those around him. Mark has been fortunate in that he has found a job within a community that has learned not to see his absence of sight as an issue. Many employers, however, are not quite so ready to act similarly.

'Basically, they just don't want to hire a blind person. Even if that person is 100 per cent qualified to do something, they are still viewed as a liability.'

Lack of sight is of course a liability, and this is something Mark readily concedes. But there are ways and means to overcome this. Being unable to see doesn't mean you are unable to do all sorts of other things. What Mark wants is for partially and severely blind people to be given a chance to prove themselves, 'in the same way that, in interview situations, everybody else has to prove themselves. You know, we are people, we are human, just like you. We might not be able to see very well, but we have other qualities and attributes that we can apply to all sorts of jobs.'

Mark's attitude to work extends to his personal life. He refuses to become restricted. He has travelled the world, challenging his disability, and encouraging everyone else to realise just how able-bodied he remains. He has trekked in Nepal, experienced the lunar landscapes of Iceland. It's Mont Blanc next. He hopes to make a documentary out of it.

I suppose this is me saying to everyone else: just don't write us off. You know, throughout my life, I have never felt that I've fully matched up to everyone else. I always felt that I had to work that little bit harder, if only to prove myself. Okay, so I don't always feel as able as the average person, but then who is the average person? So all I'm saying to people is: just give us a chance. You might be surprised.

A few days later I speak to Ian Treherne, another sight-disabled man. He tells me that Sense 'saved' him. As our conversation slowly, and falteringly, unfolds, I come to realise that he is not speaking metaphorically. We talk over Skype. He lives in Southend, where he has been, by his own admission, 'a recluse' for the last few years. He barely leaves his home, and very rarely interacts with anyone. At one point, he confesses to me that he has a phobia of even talking to people on the telephone (and this includes Skype), for the simple reason that the less he has interacted with others, the less he knows how to do so anymore. Before he answered my call this afternoon, he had to calm himself down with a cup of tea. He only agreed to my request in the first place because, he confesses, he had a good feeling.

'I sometimes get a feeling for these things. I must be an old hippy…'

Ian is 39, with long, unkempt hair, pronounced cheekbones and a wispy beard. Handsome in an angular fashion, it's difficult not to see a resemblance to the Hollywood version of Jesus Christ in him. He was born with Usher Syndrome Type 2, a condition that affects both hearing and sight. In his earlier years, he thought he was fated to remain merely deaf, because his sight was 'okay' until, abruptly, it wasn't. He was 15 when his eyesight began to fail him in ways that were not, by a long stretch, considered normal. This means that his fate was always going to be, in his words, the 'double whammy: ears and eyes. That was a kick in the nuts, let me tell you,' he scowls.

As we talk, Ian looks directly into the screen at me. There is a nervous energy to him, a tightly coiled determination I can almost reach out and touch. Much of what he says can sound defeatist, but there is a strength to him, a rage even, that suggests even in the face of defeat he will ultimately scale all the hurdles that have been aligned up before him. He is not happy about the hurdles. Losing his sight halfway through his teens was a particularly merciless cruelty. He started bumping into things, in public, at school. If he went to dark places with friends – pubs, parties – he would quickly lose them, and suddenly become alienated and lost.

Because he appears to make full eye contact while we talk, I ask him what he can see of me. He says that everything is framed within tunnel vision, but that the tiny hole at the end of that tunnel remains crystal clear. 'So I don't need glasses. Because glasses can't recreate my lost peripheral vision, unfortunately. Normal eyes have 120 degrees peripheral vision; I'm down to about 8 degrees.'

Talking to me about his blindness represents a major shift in attitude – and acceptance – for Ian. Even just a year ago, he would not have countenanced the very notion of discussing such a personal tragedy with a stranger. For the past two decades, he has been hiding his blindness from everyone, and vehemently denying it to himself. He took his driving test without telling his instructor of his condition. 'I didn't lie to him,' he points out. 'He asked me to read the numberplate in front, and I could read it perfectly.' Where his peripheral vision failed him, he simply turned his head a lot. He coped. He has a very limber neck.

He tells me that he is the product of dysfunctional parents, 'which unfortunately contributed to many of my problems to this day.' He suggests that had they been able to show him love, affection and praise, he might have learned to deal with his condition differently, better. 'I may have learned to be more strong-willed about it.' He pauses. 'But I haven't.'

His condition gradually worsened. Things became even more grave when, in 2008, the global recession hit. 'If my own blindness and deafness weren't already a kick in the nuts, the recession was an even bigger one.' He lost his job, was made redundant. He lost his flat, and because his eyesight was deteriorating rapidly by this stage, he had to relinquish the driving licence he had so protectively clung to, convinced it brought him a semblance of normality. 'Giving up the car was very hard.' And then he broke up with his girlfriend. He speaks haltingly when he tells me that, following this last event, 'everything fell apart. I had a breakdown. I was ready,' he says, 'to jump ship.'

By this he means he wanted to die. Being a practical sort of person, he scoured the internet for the best, and quickest, ways to commit suicide. 'I wanted instructions, and I found them.' It was decided: he would die by injecting heroin. He planned it all out, wrote his farewell letters, and was ready. But then, rather abruptly, he was brought up short by outside events.

'I saw a Facebook post about an old friend of mine who had just died. Suicide.' This friend, a woman who had dwarfism, had herself had struggled with issues of isolation and depression. Ian had first seen her on television confronting her issues, and felt incredibly inspired by her story. They began an email relationship, and he told her that he was about to embark upon a career as a photographer. Perhaps they could meet, and he could take her portrait? She had been keen, but Ian didn't see it through due to his own breakdown.

'And then she took her own life.'

As he tells me this, he breaks down. He brings his hands up to his eyes, impatiently brushing away the tears. 'Sorry, I didn't expect it to hit me like that. But it still hits hard, you know? Here I was ready to jump dimensions myself… and this happens.'

It shocked him, as the sheer violence of suicide on those left behind invariably does. 'It jolted me, and I suppose it also somehow put fire back into my belly.' Gradually, he began the business of living again, to have daily showers, to eat. He put weight back on, and even eventually dared to leave the house. 'Slowly, day by day, hour by hour, I was building myself up. I found that I wanted to live again, and to keep living.'

But still he felt as if he were on the very periphery of existence. He couldn't move on from this indelible fact. Among Ian's problems, he believes, is an inability to love himself, much less like himself. In a world that so summarily looked down upon those who were different, marked out in some way, the fact that he would now have to publicly acknowledge his blindness if he was ever going to live a life worth living, discomfited him. It embarrassed him.

'I was afraid of losing my identity, the identity I had tried to build up for myself over the years, as this strong, all-seeing, independent man. I didn't like the way people sounded when they said 'disabled', and so I was never going to like it when they started saying it about me.'

He began to lose himself in his photographs, taking portraits and landscapes whenever inspiration hit. He realised that he was a good photographer. He went to concerts, and crouched in the photographers' pit alongside his fellow professionals, angling his lens up at the rock star, at the sensitive folk artist. In time, he felt that this could be his new identity. He wasn't about to let it go.

Ian's photographs are as vivid as they are poignant. Many of them, either intentionally or not, seemed drenched in a kind of fog of melancholy. The foggy gloom of his New York skyline shots – before becoming reclusive, he managed to take a holiday to the US – would seem haunting even if you didn't know they were taken by an almost completely blind photographer. When you know that they are, their effect is even more overwhelming.

But this just makes him bristle. He doesn't want to be known as a blind photographer.

'It just makes people take 20 steps back, you know? I don't want to be identified in that way, and I don't feel comfortable with it.' He believes it might invoke pity.

And I don't want anybody's pity. I came across a statistic recently: 63 per cent of all people felt that they didn't have anything in common with disabled people. Sorry, but that just staggered me! [He shakes his head.] But then, to be honest, I think I knew that anyway, I just didn't *want* to know it. Because I knew that I would be treated differently, and I don't want to be treated differently.

Part of the problem, he believes, is the media. Less able-bodied people are rarely represented in the media, and when they are, it is directly *because* of their disability. They are featured in dating shows, or travel shows, and we, the viewer, are supposed to marvel at their fortitude, their inner strength, the way they grin-and-bear-it. Bless. This rankles with Ian. 'I'd like to see much more inclusion,' he says. 'The more inclusive we are, the more inclusive we will become. We'll stop seeing disparity. Besides,' he adds, 'we all have our own individual issues and challenges. Are we really so different?'

It's much as Mark Baxter had said to me. 'We are still human, still people. So why would you feel you have less in common with us?'

The more Ian Treherne came out to friends about his blindness, and about his associated fears, the more he found he lost them. His confessions alienated him because his peer group were no longer his peer group. Blindness had intervened, and his depressive fallout made them even more uncomfortable.

'Telling friends I thought I might be having a breakdown over it was very awkward indeed,' he says. 'Most of them just wanted to stick their heads in the sand until I'd stopped talking...'

He realised something many of us do at particular stages in our life: that he needed new friends. This was the point at which he reached out to Sense, during the long hangover following his breakdown. He hadn't killed himself, but this didn't mean that he particularly wanted to go on living. And even when he convinced himself that he did want to live, how was he supposed to do so now? This was a period of abject desolation. If isolation begets hopelessness, then Ian now felt hopeless: his identity had been stolen from him, or else permanently removed. Was he really so different from everybody else? Was there no one who would offer him a sympathetic ear? A way forward?

Registering himself blind should at least have been a positive practical exercise, he says, but it wasn't. 'Because I'm sorry, but the system can be cruel. To register yourself blind, to prove to them that you are blind, is fucking hard work. They put you through the wringer, and they leave you on the floor afterwards like a limp fish, barely surviving.'

It might sound like he is exaggerating somewhat here, but he insists otherwise. 'It's not just me that feels this way. I've read that loads of people have committed suicide based purely on the assessments they got. I can understand that. I came out of my own assessment a broken man, in tears. And of course something like that only contributes even further to the sense of isolation, to becoming a recluse.'

Sense helped him. At first, it did so simply by radiating empathy. The people he spoke to there were able to put him in touch with a new community of potential friends. They suggested he get a guide dog. Ian didn't want a guide dog, because what marks a blind person out to everyone else more quickly than a guide dog? The people at Sense made him see the silver lining: who doesn't love a Labrador?

'And I realised that, eventually. I'd get to have this beautiful animal, so that was a good thing.'

But the guide dog route hasn't worked out too well for Ian yet. There have been issues, and a lot of associated stress. Getting one can take years. So for now, he has to make do with the cane, which in itself is highly problematical. 'You can love a dog, but a stick? Who loves a stick?'

He has at least taken possession of one, the blind man's cane. 'It's here with me, in the flat,' he says, pointing vaguely behind him. His inner rage still roils within him, and he tries to alleviate this with gallows humour alongside depressive episodes. But with ongoing help from Sense, he is at last beginning to realise that the light at the end of his own tunnel might just be that: light.

In time, ideally, Ian might come to accept to work with what he has got, and who he is. He is a talented photographer. To become known as a *blind* photographer might be no bad calling card. Everybody needs their own calling card, and he could work with this, perhaps to his ultimate advantage. Yes, he says, nodding in agreement. That could work. He tells me that he would like to work more in the media now, or perhaps on YouTube, to help raise awareness for people like him, and help others going through what he has gone through. If he were able to do this, it would mean that he had accepted who he now is. And from this position he might be able to move forward.

He promises that he is going to use the cane soon. He will leave his flat, and step out into the brisk Southend air, a blind man making his way on the uneven pavements of his neighbourhood.

'Once I use it, the cane, that will be me having conquered it at last. It will be me standing on the top of my own Mount Everest!' He allows himself a smile.

It means I will finally embrace it, finally not give a shit. And if I can do it, if I can go out there, maybe I can help inspire other people in my situation to do it as well? That would be good, to help other people, because this has all been a huge challenge for me. I don't want challenges to stop me, I suppose because I've seen other people work around their own challenges. They've given me hope.

No longer making eye contact, peering into whatever his eyes can focus upon, real or imagined, he falls silent. I wonder what he sees.

As you can probably tell, I've found coping with my blindness fucking hard work. There is a lot of frustration. Everything takes time. There's no guidebook. But I'm ready to accept who I am. I want to be back out there in the world because I feel I'm going insane being stuck inside all the time. I miss people, a community. I miss friends.

He brushes the hair from his eyes, and tamps down his beard. I ask him when will it happen? When will he take his cane out? When will he accept his status, and resume the business of his life?

He considers the question for so long I wonder whether our internet connection has gone. But, no, he's still there. He is considering his answer.

'Soon,' he says.

Several months later, I hear from Ian again. He sends me a photograph of himself with it, the cane, the dreaded cane. It stands tall and proud, somehow, alongside him. It does not look out of place. 'Quite a few months of brain pain,' he texts, 'but I'm now using my cane all the time. It's changed my life.'

Directory

Sense

https://www.sense.org.uk/

0300 330 9250

Scope

https://www.scope.org.uk

0808 800 3333

ELEVEN

The refugee crisis

For a refugee, Diana Saif has had it, in her words, 'easy'. Everything is relative, of course, but what this young woman has been through in her short life could hardly be justifiably described as that. True, she didn't make her way from Syria overland, on foot, through Turkey and any successive border control it might have been possible to slip through unchecked under the cover of night, and nor did she sail from the coast of Africa or Greece towards Lampedusa and mainland Italy crammed into a sinking rubber dinghy alongside people who might once have been her neighbours. She did not arrive in the UK unable to speak the language, without friends, a modest support network, or without certain means and resources.

This is what constitutes just how *easy* she has had it, how lucky she has been.

Before the war in Syria, her parents, both architects, would have been viewed as middle-class and comfortable. They had a nice house, a disposable income, three children whose education they could pay for. But when peaceful demonstrations in 2011 were met with government forces, the country was turned into a war state by 2012, and all sense of comfort vanished. Whatever would happen next for them would be uncharted territory. They would have to start again, elsewhere.

Diana had arrived in the UK before the war broke out. She was in London to complete her Masters degree. When the fighting began, she found herself overnight an asylum seeker. She and her then husband were unable to return to their country of birth, not merely because it was no longer safe to do so, but because her husband would have been conscripted into obligatory military service. In order to remain in England, even temporarily, they required valid passports. Hers was fine, but his was close to expiring. Returning to Damascus to renew it would have been a fool's errand; he'd never have been allowed back out again. Instead, over Christmas 2012, they flew to Beirut in the hope of navigating the necessary bureaucracy from there. With ignorance comes blind optimism.

It was, Diana says now, 'a hopeless case. We came back to London, and applied for asylum at the airport. The life we had known, the life we had built together – gone, just like that.'

There is an exacting procedure for asylum seekers when arriving in Great Britain. If you have no ready accommodation, and Diana and her husband didn't, you are sent to an initial accommodation centre. Diana and her husband were sent to one in Wakefield, West Yorkshire. 'A horrible experience,' she says. Situated as it was alongside a prison, with its high walls and barbed wire, it was difficult for them not to feel that they were classified as prisoners themselves.

Day-to-day life is severely restricted in accommodation centres like this one. Here, they were fed two meals a day, and given bunkbeds in a shared bedroom. They had no access to their bank accounts – which held in the region of £700 – until their case had been processed and checked, and this, they were assured, could take a while. There were curfews, lights out at a certain hour. You can see what Diana means when she says that they felt like prisoners. This was surely no way for the blameless – for victims – to live, and she felt this abrupt change of life acutely, all its prior freedoms and opportunities replaced by supervised mealtimes in impersonal canteens that smelled of mass-produced food and cleaning agents. The atmosphere in such places is unavoidably grim, surrounded by people whose own life stories have been freshly collapsed into something unrecognisable. Abject misery hangs like fog, and the collective sense of dislocation often feeds into a festering discontent.

Initial accommodation centres are hardly welcoming places. This isn't to criticise the UK's clearing process for asylum seekers – which can hardly be an easy thing; and if they are located close to prisons it is because land close to prisons is cheaper than land close to shopping centres and Royal Parks – but while you are being processed for asylum status, you inevitably become less human and more statistic. It's a matter of efficiency.

Diana had become a statistic. Life slowed to a standstill, her studies put on hold, forbidden from taking any employment. She spent her days wondering what would happen next, where fate might lead them. She hardly slept, and was perpetually exhausted.

'The whole thing was a very traumatising experience,' she says. 'And it took a long time to process it, to accept and understand what was happening to us, and why.'

If she did manage to process it, she did so simply by comparing her levels of trauma to those of her fellow countrymen and women whose own collective plight was by now making the headline news daily. 'In 2015, when we read that people were walking across Europe, literally walking across it, and swimming and drowning in the sea – well, then I realised how insignificant our own experience was, how fortunate we were.'

They remained in the accommodation centre for three weeks before being granted a temporary discharge, refugee status still pending. At this point they were permitted partial access to their bank account, and the giddy freedom to find their own place to stay in and around the Greater Wakefield area. Keep your receipts, they were told. When their money ran out, they would be re-admitted into the centre for another indeterminate amount of time.

But Diana had no intention of returning. 'We decided we were never going to go back there,' she says. Instead, they travelled to Bradford, where they stayed with a friend, then moved back down to London and sofa-surfed with people they had met while studying there the previous year.

What happened next further suggests how 'lucky' Diana was. The science firm where she had had work experience while studying for her Masters, and which has a large multi-national workforce, offered her a full-time job once she had attained refugee status, and in time she would be granted a five-year visa to remain in the UK. Though her marriage would ultimately suffer from the compounded stress of everything they had gone through – she and her husband split up – she thrived in the job and moved into a pleasant suburb of London, now within easy reach of Royal Parks, an ample Waitrose. Though she continued to live with the shadow of war, she settled. Years passed.

A week after we meet, she is granted indefinite leave to remain. 'I can now stay in the UK with no expiry date,' she says, 'and will be eligible to apply for citizenship in 12 months.' Good news, notionally, though all she really wants, and still craves, is to return to the life she had known in Syria.

'There are moments, every day, when I think to myself: why does it all have to be so much effort? Why can't I just be back at home in a coffee shop that I like? But you can't think like that for too long. If you do, you'll end up in bed again for a week. You'll go to the doctor again asking for more antidepressants.'

She then does that thing that people who have endured so much do in a vain attempt to somehow ameliorate it: she smiles.

Now 30, Diana exerts the kind of resolve you only ever see in people who have been required to strengthen theirs due to unavoidable chaos. We meet in a café in south-west London over the Easter weekend, during her lunch hour. 'I work a lot.' Her English is perfect, and she speaks it in a commanding voice that cuts through the clatter of IKEA spoons on cheap crockery, prompting people at nearby tables to eavesdrop, clearly fascinated by the tale she tells. Were we in another part of the country, she suggests, she might have to lower her voice. Not everyone wants asylum seekers on their doorstep. But then even multi-cultural cities are never entirely safe.

'True story,' she says. 'I was in the supermarket recently, and somebody looked at me and asked me where I was from.

When I told her Syria, she asked if I was a terrorist.' She has expressive eyebrows, Diana, perhaps more so than most of us, for the simple fact that she has so much to express. They convey consternation now. 'I just looked at her and said, *Really?*'

It isn't easy to find refugees to talk about what it's like to be a refugee. They are wary of outside interest, and the possible motivations behind it. They wonder what benefit it is for them to share their awful stories with yet more strangers. A great many don't want to tell their stories because, Diana explains, they can't. It's too painful, too raw, still very much in the present tense. They don't trust themselves to talk without suffering another balefully routine spike in anxiety levels, cortisol raging, tears. Diana says that she couldn't talk about her own experiences for at least her first three years in London, a subject she couldn't broach out loud. Which made everyday exchanges with friends complicated.

'When work colleagues asked about my family, how they were back home, I appreciated the compassion, of course I did, but I just didn't want to go there, I couldn't.'

Though she says she is prepared to talk to me now, a palpable suspicion remains. She is wary about how I will convey her on the page, the quotes I will suggest that come from her mouth. She has to be careful, she stresses. If she is seen to be critical about the Assad regime, it could put her, and family members, in danger. 'Diana Saif' is not her real name.

She explains that refugees have come to believe that their host countries have reached a peak of 'refugee fatigue'. We have heard too much about them and their sorry plight by now; we've our own issues to worry about. The mass exodus of migrants across Europe has dominated the headlines for so long that it's all become just so much white noise.

In parallel, the asylum seekers themselves prefer increasingly to keep themselves to themselves.

'From our perspective, the reality of things on the ground is that nothing much is changing,' she says. 'There is a lot of media talk, yes, and a lot of charities doing fundraising, which is good, but the impact we feel on the ground is not always as significant as we might have hoped it would be. So when people talk to us about our situation, how they might help, it's hard for us to know what else to say.'

Nevertheless, a great many charities – and individuals – are actively working hard to deal with their plight, to make them feel more at home in a land that all-too self-evidently isn't, and to reduce their sense of isolation. Several of the charities I contact tell me that they continually strive to override any refugee fatigue the collective 'we' might be feeling for the simple fact that the fatigue isn't real at all, but rather a media construct, a political football.

Mariam Kemple Hardy, the head of campaigns at Refugee Action in London, says that they are inundated with calls on a daily basis from people wanting to know what they can do, how they can help. They are appalled, she tells me, at how refugees have been portrayed in certain sections of the media, and by certain political parties, and they are adamant to show that this isn't representative of the rest of us, of most of us. Most of us, they insist, want to help. Tell us how.

Alongside charities doing similar work, Refugee Action's aims are to make the unimaginable bearable for those who do arrive into the UK from Syria, and Afghanistan, and elsewhere. They meet them at the ports and the airports, and arrange their first hot meal. They work with housing providers to get them appropriate accommodation. They source schools for children, and English classes for adults. They work with local communities in coming together to form voluntary welcome groups that support newly arrived refugees to get to know their new neighbourhoods, where, they say, people are ready to greet them, to facilitate, wherever possible, integration.

Kemple Hardy tells me:

Ever since the world woke up to the refugee crisis, we've just had the most overwhelming response from the public. Yes, there are pockets of discontent, and often across social media, but the reaction on the ground has been nothing but positive and proactive. It is an enormous problem, of course, the refugee crisis, and some people can feel a little overwhelmed by it, but the moment you react to it on a human level, then you know what to do: you reach out and offer to help. It doesn't matter how small the effort is – inviting refugees to dance nights, to the local town hall, to cuisine sharing – it counts, because what we are trying to do here is build communities, new communities.

This, in effect, is what Diana has managed to do herself. She has built herself a new community. Her siblings are living close by, and she has recently brought her mother over to live here. Her father continues to shuttle between London and

Damascus, where the extended family still lives. It is never an easy journey. Diana has also become part of an online initiative that encourages migrants from all over the world to post essays on any subject they feel moved to write about: memories of home, mostly. 'The Land We Once Had' is the title of one post. Another talks about their hometown, where the local produce is aubergines. 'I feel sad when I hear that my hometown is changing,' the author writes. 'Everything is new. It does not match the identity of the town in my memory, where the houses were made of black stones. I feel sad because I was forced to leave.'

The writing is vivid and tangible, and it keeps the diaspora connected in crucially tangible ways.

This, Diana explains, is wholly necessary.

And that's because people like me, they carry trauma. They carry a toxic level of stress with them. It's something we have to live with on a daily basis. We have left a conflict zone, our families, our childhood homes behind. We don't know if we'll ever go back, if we'll ever be able to – if we want to, even, after the destruction has ended. So this is all very stressful. Then, alongside all this, we have to try to fit into this new community, we have to start to live a new life from scratch. It doesn't matter where we have come from, what our credentials may be, our qualifications or work experiences, because we are just back to Square Zero. I have worked very hard to get my job, and to keep the job, and I have been lucky to work for a very understanding company, and to have a very sympathetic boss. But dealing with it all, on a daily basis – this still requires a massive effort.

One reason why integration is quite so complicated is because in some sense, the refugees never really fully leave home, at least not in the psychological sense. They remain addicted to news alerts and updates, mostly fed to them via social media. Every time their phones vibrate, more bad news is delivered. It is difficult to be in the here and now when you have just had word that a bomb has been dropped near Damascus, where so many people you know, people you have grown up with and loved, continue to live.

The dehumanisation of this war is the worst thing. What we once considered unacceptable increasingly becomes acceptable the longer the war goes on. You come to accept the living conditions of the people you know back home – the fact that there is no hot water for showers, little electricity, hardly any Internet, and that jobs don't exist in the way they did before – and you also come to accept death. That is particularly horrible. It's got to the stage now where, when we hear that someone has died, we need to know *how* they died before we know how to react to it. If they have died from illness, they are considered one of the fortunate ones; there is less trauma to deal with for us after a natural death.

People sometimes wonder why we have so much anger and frustration. This is why.

I ask her about the charitable initiatives aiming to help people in her situation, whether they help. Do they make a difference? Do they in some small way ease the collective suffering? Is there more that can be done? Her answer is complicated. Yes, she says, of course it helps, and they are grateful for it. But still, many of her friends have struggled. They haven't been lucky as she has to remain in a big cosmopolitan city, and instead have been sent elsewhere in the country, into smaller towns and villages which might not be quite as multicultural, and where refugees - who often don't speak a word of English - might not be quite so welcomed, and will therefore struggle.

'But,' she says, smiling, 'as Tesco puts it: every little helps. If people are genuinely interested in helping out, then volunteer. Volunteer for one of the many charities, for Refugee Action, for the Cook for Syria initiative [where people come together to celebrate Syrian cuisine and raise money to help UNICEF protect Syrian children]. Offer to host asylum seekers and refugees, make them feel like they are welcome, especially because the media is constantly bombarding them with hateful messages.'

The best thing anybody can do, she says, is to help recent arrivals learn English. 'It's been thoroughly researched, and this is the best thing you can do because language is the largest barrier. You overcome that barrier, and life becomes much easier. So, help teach English, because it is a lovely thing to do. But please,' she adds, 'don't pity us. Nobody coming from any culture wants to feel pity. Our dignity is compromised when we feel your pity. Instead, I would say that it is so much better to show care, love even.'

For a moment, Diana is quiet. 'Compassion,' she says, at last. 'That's the word I'm looking for. Compassion. To receive compassion from people, that's a great feeling. The best feeling.'

I ask Diana to tell me about initiatives that she has been involved with, and she tells me about Nottingham, where they set up a four-day workshop to introduce recent arrivals to the community at large. They invited down anyone who might want to come.

And many people did – local authors, active community members, people who worked in the museum. What was so great about this was that we simply threw people together around a table of food – and two facilitators to guide them – and that's it! That's all the integration we really need, I think, because things like this can have amazing results. In Nottingham, none of the Syrians spoke English, and none of the English, of course, spoke Arabic, but they held a workshop together over four days – I was there to interpret – and at the end of the workshop, everyone involved put on an entire storytelling and musical evening together. I tell you, it was *mesmerising*.

So that is Diana's advice: teach English, host workshops, offer up tables full of food. People will connect, because people always do. It's no quick fix, and it might well fracture long-term, but these are difficult situations, perhaps impossible for some. But it's a start. The more such initiatives occur, she believes, the easier the transition. And then perhaps more people will go on to find their feet in this way, and with it a certain stability, and might ultimately follow a narrative like Diana's, a refugee becoming a resource, a member of the community, still very much herself, a woman with her own identity, her own past and her own future, but nevertheless one of us.

Reaching out to refugees, of course, benefits more than just the refugees themselves. This isn't one-way traffic. As much as the former benefits, so do the hosts themselves.

Refugees at Home is a charity that matches people fleeing turmoil from around the world with individuals in the UK who have a spare room, or even a sofa bed, to offer. Sara Nathan, a co-founder and trustee of Refugees at Home, tells me that the offer of something as simple as temporary bed and board is a key component towards ultimate integration, and Diana Saif might likely agree. Those asylum seekers that do achieve refugee status are given leave to remain in the UK for five years, but, Nathan says, 'this is the point at which they are evicted from their asylum centre, and it takes more than the 28 days' grace to get a National Insurance number, and then a legal job and bank account benefits, so recent refugees also struggle to find accommodation.'

It is this stark reality that leads to a rather shocking statistic: 81 per cent of those given refugee status go on to become destitute. 'They've suffered the persecution of war, they've managed to get permission to stay in the UK, but then they are slung out onto the street. It doesn't make very much sense to me.'

Refugees at Home was set up in 2015, and has so far made over 1000 placements. Most of the people they host are men between the ages of 18 and 30, and though volunteers come from all sorts of backgrounds, and are young and old alike, a disproportionate number of those who offer up their homes tend to be Jewish, Quaker and/or gay. Who knows why, says Nathan, but perhaps these are people who have suffered persecution themselves, and consequently empathise. The criteria to become a host are pleasingly un-bureaucratic. Hosts are not allowed to charge rent or otherwise exploit their guests, and if they are offering a house that contains several people – a typical nuclear family, for example – then every member has to be on board. 'This is because many of these people have come from a war zone. We don't want to introduce them to another one.'

The accommodation itself doesn't have to be particularly luxurious, and in some cases that aforementioned sofa bed really will suffice. 'As long as it's more comfortable than a park bench or a graveyard, then it should be fine.' Some stay for a week, others longer. The average is 46 days. Lasting friendship is often formed. Only very rarely, Nathan suggests, do the pairings not work out.

'We've only had one incident where we had to report someone to Prevent, the anti-terrorism organisation – and that was most likely, we think, actually a mental health problem.' And of all the very many placements, only a couple of people have transgressed by propositioning their hosts, and only a couple of hosts have transgressed by propositioning their guests. Mostly, they get on because, mostly, people do.

Inevitably, the charity has more refugees than places to house them, and they are always looking for more volunteers. Nathan argues that it has proven such a popular scheme because those who do arrive here really do want to understand how their host country works, they want to learn the language, to integrate. In those cases where refugees are housed separately, together, where they only speak in Arabic, then the chances for integration exponentially diminish. They remain cocooned, in bubbles. What they need, and in many cases actively seek, is exposure, and opportunity.

'Who wants young men with no access to education, not allowed to work, no money, who just hang about the place all the time?' Sara Nathan says. 'Nobody. It's bonkers. You want people to be gainfully employed, involved in society, in education – and that is what we are striving to help create here.'

And as it is created, and subsequently fostered, loneliness is combated on both sides. 'Many people who live alone would much rather have somebody else rattling around their empty houses with them,' she says. And of the lodgers themselves: 'Well, it's unlikely that they will feel as antagonistic towards British society as perhaps they might otherwise feel if people are going to such effort to welcome them, right?'

It is always nice, in cases like this, to have a pleasing example to help illustrate the point, and Nathan offers me one now. She recounts the story of a 78-year-old woman, one of their volunteer hosts, who rather unfortunately fell under a tube train at Notting Hill Gate station in London one day. A tiny lady, and fragile with it, she was lucky not to die given the injuries she sustained. While paramedics attempted to prise her free from beneath the train, they were sure one of her legs would have to be amputated. But she was lucky, because ultimately she was saved, limbs intact.

'Though she did spend the next five weeks bedridden in hospital, with a crushed pelvis, a broken leg, broken ribs. And all she wanted to do was go home.' Doctors were hardly likely to grant her request, an infirm pensioner to convalesce home alone. Except they did. 'She had a houseguest, a Syrian man who just happened to be a doctor. So,' she says in optimistic summation, 'you see, it really does work both ways. Everybody benefits.'

Directory

British Red Cross
https://www.redcross.org.uk/
0344 871 11 11

Refugee Action
https://www.refugee-action.org.uk/
0845 894 2536

Refugees at Home
https://www.refugeesathome.org

Twelve

The circle of life

It affects everyone, then, all of us, of every ability and configuration, at every stage of our lives, in every chapter, for a multiplicity of reasons. It comes and it goes, it stays and it lingers, and it can threaten to ruin everything until we seek some kind of help, be it medical, professional or philanthropic. But where loneliness comes clattering to its final halt, where it sets up its stall with the cruel promise of going nowhere any time soon, is back to where we began: at the end.

The end of life is where loneliness roosts longest, determined to colour our final years into swatches of greys and blacks. As medicine appears determined to keep us living longer, more and more of us will end up in care homes eventually, venues where loneliness plays its melancholic tune each evening. There can be few places as dispiriting to enter as a care home for the elderly. Even in the very best examples, they are little more than waiting rooms largely devoid of vim and vitality, the reasonable assumption that vim and vitality are ingredients that have long since expired. It is possible, of course, that many new entrants might just welcome the mausoleum quiet – a percentage, at least, will be tired and ill; after a lifetime of noise, they might crave nothing more than the library-like atmosphere of perpetual whispers – but statistics show that an active mind is key to mental health. Statistics also suggest that there is no reason why we cannot keep a hold of our active minds until the very end. The more a care home actually does feel like the ultimate waiting room, the worse it is for those who have to spend extended amounts of time in them.

What they all need, then, is a rethink, a different approach. Why not liven them up a little, and see what happens?

Judith Ish-Horowicz, a teacher who was awarded an MBE in 2010 for Services to Early Years Education, has run a nursery in south London for the past quarter-century, and now runs one within the grounds of a care home. It is the first of its kind in the UK, and the trumpet it blows is a loud one. It's like no other care home you have ever seen before; it's full of life. Judith tells me she always found it curious that, when we reach a certain stage in life, we stop interacting with older people outside of our own family members. The consequence of this is that they quickly become to us a demographic we go out of our way to avoid.

'But I'm convinced it's a fairly modern problem, and a fairly Western one at that,' she says. 'Families across Asia, for example, tend to stay together much more, either due to traditional values or else restrictive finances that do not allow younger generations to splinter off towards independent living.'

And not just Asia. Travel to any Mediterranean resort during the summer months, and you will see countless local examples of three, sometimes four, generations of the same family beached beneath the same sun umbrella. But nuclear families are increasingly the norm in the UK, which means not only that there is more space under our sun umbrellas, but that children have precious few relationships with older people.

For 25 years, Judith was convinced that the younger generation was missing out on something crucial to their development. And so, 10 times a year, she endeavoured to do something about it by bringing her pre-school charges to Nightingale House, a long-established care home in Wandsworth, for some intergenerational interaction. Each visit proved such a success that, Judith says, she lamented the fact that they couldn't do it more often, 'if not all the time.'

Her conviction percolated away steadily, and remained undimmed. In 2017, she was at last able to do something about it.

At 10 o'clock every morning, the Apples & Honey nursery here within Nightingale House enjoys an hour and a half of shared play. Today, it's some pointedly highbrow play: an intimate piano recital comprising the greatest hits of Bach and Beethoven, delivered by an Anglo-Chinese pianist with a winningly determined commitment to her craft. Her tenacity is required because her audience today, split evenly between the over 80s and the under fives, is surely not as attentive as she is used to playing before. Several in the former camp do listen on with rapt wonder, though it is also true to say that others are nodding off; in the latter camp, the toddlers are behaving the way toddlers have every right to. Several, sat in the laps of their carers, are asking their carers questions, and pointing things out, and breaking off into songs of their own. Were it any quieter in here, we might hear Beethoven spinning in his grave. One small child cries briefly; another has a finger up his nose. Beside me, an elderly woman takes the whole thing in. The smile on her face is as bright as the strip lighting above.

It is, by any measure, a completely delightful scene: fun, engaging, and fully interactive. The pianist, coming to the end of what she might know as a sonata, stands and takes a bow. She has earned her applause, and everybody does indeed clap appreciatively, even the child who has at last removed his digit from his nostril. But Ali Somers, the co-founder of this care home/nursery initiative, takes me to one side to confess in a whisper that, from her perspective, it's a failure, and a potential health and safety nightmare: too many people, not enough space, scant organisation. She will be sending emails about this later, she says, with the suggestion that, going forward, group activities will be required to display more evident forethought.

As the fleeting severity of her frown suggests, the running of an institution that pairs the very old with the very young may be an objectively brilliant idea on so many levels, and one that elicits positive consequences for all concerned, but it is also one hell of a logistical headache.

Ali, who is lovely and enthusiastic, an open book, says: 'We are learning as we go along. And we very much believe in full transparency, so that we – and others – can learn from what we are doing.'

It was in September 2017 that Judith Ish-Horowicz's long nurtured dream at last came true, when the nursery opened its doors here. Judith is its principal. There are 200 residents in Nightingale House, and 400 staff, which gives every indication needed that this is perhaps better than the average care home. The addition of a nursery full of small children with boundless energy levels and low centres of gravity is only as problematical as the staff allow it to be, and the staff appear so capably efficient in their day-to-day work that it hasn't been very problematical at all.

Set at the end of its own lush gardens, a gentle walk from the main building and its residents, Apples & Honey finds itself in an area of pleasant, even rural-aping beauty – the garden is manicured; there are fish in the pond, birds in the trees – and the children are frequent guests at the big house, where they walk through in an attention-grabbing crocodile line, from one pre-school event to the next.

The big house's residents, Ali Somers explains, are always pleased to see them. Well, she adds quickly, not all of them. 'Some of the residents no longer want to be around young children, and that is absolutely fine. There is only interaction if they want it. But many, we find, do.'

If care homes typically revolve around the whole idea of the end of life, then this is an initiative that focuses instead on lives still being very actively lived. If the project takes off, then this could – and should – be the future.

The care home, which was founded 170 years ago, sits in a quiet corner of Wandsworth, south London. If it looks big from the outside, and it does, it's even bigger inside, sprawling with corridors that seem to go on for ever. But for a building that houses as many as 600 people, both residents and staff, it is eerily quiet and unaccountably efficient. Where is everybody? Many of the older people are in their rooms, each equipped with an ensuite and TV. Others can be found in the little nooks and crannies located at the end of the carpeted corridors, indulging in communal activities, reading books, or else sleeping off their last meal. Staircases and lifts take you up and down into other parts of the building, which themselves appear to be connected to yet further annexes. You don't get from A to B here without first passing through L, M, N and O. It pays to be content to amble. Walking through the place, feet silent on the staticky carpet below, you are put in mind of a slow-going ocean liner, where the destination is not as important as the journey towards it.

As many municipal buildings do, Nightingale House has its own motto, theirs refreshingly not in Latin: *From generation to generation*. The connection between the generations is what's important. Bringing the old and the young together, Judith Ish-Horowicz believed, would aid interaction, would form unlikely but tenacious bonds. It might even, they hoped, lift the very spirit of the place itself. And, according to Ali Somers, it really has.

'The feedback we've received from residents and parents alike has been resoundingly positive,' she says.

A busy café area at the front of the building is where everyone congregates. It is here, each lunchtime, that mothers and fathers stream through on their way to collect their charges, alongside nannies and sundry relatives, many of whom will stop for coffee and a bite to eat with whomever they find there. It's like a John Lewis restaurant: cordoned-off coves are littered with prams and strollers that jostle for space alongside empty wheelchairs and walking frames. Every few minutes, another crocodile line of children stumbles smilingly by, making exultant noise.

On the morning I visit, at the end of the classical concert, half a dozen of the residents make slow progress to another floor, reached by a distant lift, for another regular Monday morning event, the Jewish ceremony of Havdalah, which recognises the end of Shabbat (the Sabbath) and readies people for the working week ahead. This is a deliberately child-friendly occasion that revolves around the (supervised) lighting of a candle, and so after the residents, all of them women today, have taken their seats in the appointed room, in come the children. A headcount is problematical for the simple reason that they don't sit still for long enough, but there must be at least 10 of them. They sit on the floor, except for one of them, Daisy, who for some reason is busy performing a downward dog pose. Judith leads them all into religious song. (While Nightingale House residents are Jewish, the children are of all faiths, or often no faith at all.)

At one point, a small boy, Eddie, is abruptly whisked off at speed to the toilet, suddenly fearful he might wet himself. When he returns, minutes later, mercifully dry and proud of it, everybody sings him 'Happy Birthday'. He is three years old today. 'Me,' he points out, in clarification.

The service lasts an eventful half hour, after which the children hug the old women in turn, and the women beam back with untrammelled pleasure. 'See you next week,' they trill.

There is much in common, Ali tells me, between those in the early stages of dementia and very young children. And so they are, in a sense, perfect playmates. Each lives fully in the present, and often has to be reminded of the other's existence. Research in similar initiatives around the world has shown that older people are happier, and more alert, when around young children. Even those with advanced Alzheimer's, who might otherwise struggle with communication skills, find they can speak in coherent sentences when holding a baby, and can remember the words to lullabies they haven't sung in decades.

'Having these children close by, and interacting with them, makes them feel like part of a community again,' Ali says. 'They tell me they love to watch the children as they problem-solve, as they grow over the weeks and months. It makes them feel that they are taking a stake in the child's development. It revives them, it really does.'

Any of the problems one might imagine occurring in such a situation simply don't arise. There is no awkwardness felt on either side. This is because children don't see any discernible difference in those many years older than themselves. They do not see the wheelchairs, the limitations, the infirmity. 'They just see someone else to play with, someone else to give them attention. Which in many ways is what we all crave, don't we?'

The idea of placing nursery-aged children within the grounds of an elderly care home first originated in Japan in the 1970s. Two decades later, there were almost 20 schemes across the country, and their success was later replicated in the US and Canada. Now there are similar intergenerational schemes in Europe, and if Apples & Honey Nightingale is the first of its kind in the UK, it will be joined by others soon enough. The more clearly beneficial the scheme, the quicker it will get picked up and adopted elsewhere.

Stephen Burke is the coordinator of an initiative called United for All Ages, which aims to build stronger communities and a stronger UK by bringing its young and old together. It was started, he explains, because of what he saw as an 'age apartheid'.

'There is increasing segregation between the different age groups in our society.' He goes on to point out that this wasn't always the case. 'Certainly not. If you look back in time, there are lots of examples of our generations being much more together in lots of different ways. But in the last 30–40 years, for all sorts of different reasons, the respective age groups have become segregated, particularly so for the oldest and youngest.'

To many, this might seem not particularly problematical. What, after all, do those at the beginning of life have in common with those at its tail end? But the benefits of integration, Burke insists, run both ways. The more fractured the country becomes – and after Brexit, it has started to feel less fractured than cleanly broken in half – the more we become alienated from one another. The more alienated we remain, the more we will continue to misunderstand each other, convinced we are all poles apart when, in fact, the truth might be quite the opposite.

'Age apartheid leads to any number of issues,' he says. 'Loneliness, isolation, a lack of mutual understanding, possible mistrust, and stereotyping. It all just polarises society, and that isn't to society's benefit. If we mixed more, there would be more positive outcomes for all concerned, because we would be tackling ageing better. We would be tackling the different ways the generations view one another, and we would also begin to realise how many commonalities there are.'

Not all old people are out of touch, much as not every young person with a wardrobe almost comprising exclusively of hoodies is up to no good. 'The debunking of stereotypes is no bad thing,' he asserts.

And so the benefits of opening up a care home to nurseries, he believes, are myriad. There have been many studies to suggest that social interaction decreases loneliness, but also delays mental decline in general. It lowers blood pressure, reduces the risk of disease and death in elders. One Japanese study from 2013 even showed that socialising across generations increases the amount of smiling and conversation in older adults. Moods lift.

But it also improves the quality of care itself for those residents. By their very nature, care homes are closed institutions; you only enter if you really have to. Consequently, not all of the assistance on offer is always up to standard. By opening them up, more eyes would be trained upon them; there would be more people around. Stephen Burke believes it would help challenge the staff, but also keep them engaged.

'One of the wonderful things about Nightingale House is that the café and restaurant area is open, so there are constantly people visiting, there is constant interaction. This means that everyone remains more engaged, and connected.'

And if the older people are benefiting from this, their younger counterparts are, too. Getting children to mix with older people in varying states of frailty and dementia, and so on, is probably going to change their entire life perspective on aging, and on older people. They will learn to socialise with those outside their immediate peer group, and though they may not fully appreciate it at the time, they get to see the very arc of life. That has to be beneficial.

Reports have shown that, while children do forge close bonds with the older people, they don't react as badly to their inevitable deaths as one might expect. Studies at a similar initiative in Seattle, Providence Mount, have shown that while children certainly notice a resident's sudden absence, and enquire about them, they demonstrated little significant emotional attachment. There are still other residents there to make a fuss of them, after all. They move on, which must play a significant role in the development of emotional maturity.

The unambiguous success of these early initiatives is being noted. In 2017, a school in east London opened its doors to older people with dementia and depression issues for three days a week, where they shared in group activities with Reception class pupils. In Cambridge, there is a sheltered housing scheme in which some of the flats are let to postgraduate students at a reduced rent in return for 30 hours of volunteering a month. In Singapore, $3 billion is being invested in similar shared projects, a governmental response to an ageing population, and realising that quality of life is something we all deserve, however old we might grow to be. (It might also be worth pointing out that such shared profits would be less financially draining on the state; not all governmental initiatives are altruistic.)

'When I'm 80, I want the world to be a better place for all of us,' says Stephen Burke. 'So anything that improves the level of care, and the outlook, of care homes can only be a good thing, as far as I am concerned.'

Directory

Nightingale House
https://www.nightingalehammerson.org

United for All Ages
https://unitedforallages.com/

Livability
https://www.livability.org.uk/
020 7452 2000

THIRTEEN

How to ~~dis~~connect

Three years ago, the cat that had asserted squatters' rights in our house and treated it as his own was knocked down by a car for the last time. We missed the calm authority he exerted over family mealtimes, the way he brought us all together. Arguments were swiftly diffused when Billy was in residence. If my wife wasn't yet home from work – my wife a woman who believes that an animal's place is never upon the kitchen table – Billy would take his rightful place upon the kitchen table, watching with detached interest as my daughters and I made our way through dinner, confident that the spoils would be kept for him.

After his death, my girls pleaded that in some respectful way we replace Billy with another animal, one of our own. A dog. We had long wanted to get a dog, but had held off in due deference to Billy. But with the cat now gone, there was nothing to stop us.

Two years later, and Missy, an energetic Border Terrier, is an intrinsic part of our lives, an occasional diversion for the children, a full-time one for us. My wife does the morning walk, while I take the mid-afternoon slot. Walking the dog gets me out of the house more; my wife tells me this is good. She had been worried by my own deepening sense of professionally prompted isolation, and insisted it would be beneficial to interact with other human beings from time to time.

As ever, my wife was right: the dog has brought me out of a shell I never fully realised I was living deep within. As a lifelong city dweller, I'm used to being unfriendly and standoffish to everyone, not talking to the neighbours, never broaching a conversation on a tube or train. I would occasionally make exceptions on transatlantic flights, but only with Americans, because Americans rarely stop talking. Context, for an embedded Londoner, is everything. While I am still unlikely to find the appropriate words to exchange with people in the post office queue, I will happily talk to pretty much any dog that arrives in the park with their owner at the end of a leash. Context. It's the dog that permits the conversation to start; the fresh air that surrounds us provides the follow-through oxygen. I will go to the park for half an hour and come back 90 minutes later, having lost track of the time and enjoyed more meaningful conversations with dog owners – whose names I very often fail to learn – than I have had with friends for years. There is the part-time actress and reluctant nanny; the narcoleptic window cleaner who likes to describe himself as 'the village idiot'; the entrepreneurial Indonesian, the Indian widow. The mother of an autistic son; the other mother whose own son is currently doing trials with Wimbledon FC. The early retiree with psoriasis and arthritis whose Bulldog can dribble a basketball the way Messi does a football.

Some have revealed to me their secrets, confessions and yearnings, their transgressions with the law. I've shared plenty of my own. Some connections have become unaccountably deep, three laps of the park all that's required to encourage full disclosure of matters intimate and private. Until we got the dog, I thought my ability to talk to strangers had receded badly with age. It is sometimes profoundly pleasurable to be proved wrong.

One of the park regulars, Louise, knew that another of the regulars, David, was going to be all alone at Christmas. David had already told me that he was alone by choice: a big extended family gathering was looming for New Year, but David, who lived alone with his malodorous Mastiff, was perfectly content to watch the Queen's speech by himself. David is close to 60, Louise in her early 80s. David walked his dog on that day at its usual time, and inevitably he bumped into a few of the regulars, Louise among them. In Louise's hand was a plastic bag around which the dogs were fussily gathering. Laughing, David wondered if she had brought with her some Christmas lunch.

She had, but the remains – neatly secured in a Tupperware box, slices of turkey breast on a bed of potatoes and vegetables – weren't for the dogs, they were for David, whom she knew was not much of a cook. 'A late lunch,' Louise had told him. 'Seasons greetings.'

When David, a man as gruff as his Mastiff, recounted this story to me afterwards, his eyes shone with tears. Caught off guard by them, he turned to face the wind. We walked on, our dogs at our heels.

While this gentle act of kindness was happening on Christmas afternoon, I was in a pub, the Alexandria, in Wimbledon, south-west London. The Alexandria is a handsome place that, in the way of all twenty-first-century pubs, has ideas above its station, creeping as it is stealthily into a local restaurant of note. Christmas lunch at the Alexandria, £80 a head, sells out months in advance. But six years ago, landlord Mick Dore and his wife Sarah became increasingly concerned that many of their Christmas Day clientele – not those gorging themselves in the restaurant but rather those propping up the bar, alone – were there for a pertinent reason. 'Though they would never admit it themselves,' Mick told me, 'they were lonely. I felt for them. We all did.'

He had an idea. How about dividing the restaurant in two: half for paying guests, while the other half – those alone on the day itself – would be invited in for a meal on the house? Simply turn up at any time between midday and three, no booking required, to be served a three-course meal, a drop of alcohol, and a few pulls on a few crackers. Six years later, their idea has gathered some impressive momentum, having trended on Twitter and landed on the desks of newspapers keen to write good news for a change.

Local businesses also took note, and now generously donate barrels of beer, crates of wine and as many turkeys as required. Individuals have even approached him wanting to donate money, but Mick has no need for charitable donations. He tells me he has been pleasantly surprised by the benevolence of all involved.

'They just want to help out. You'd be surprised how many do.'

When I arrive at the pub, on what is surely the warmest Christmas Day since last Christmas Day – freezing festivities a thing of the past in a globally warmed London – it is a little before midday. I arrive alongside at least half a dozen volunteers, who are here via social media. Mick welcomes them, these singletons in their 30s and 40s who work, I learn, in industries like graphic design and HR, and are, for various private reasons, alone themselves today. He walks them around the pub, shows them the kitchen, the tables, the loos.

'No idea how many people might be turning up,' Mick says to them. 'Could be 50, could be 500. But we'll be busy, so have a drink first and get yourself in the mood.'

I find I'm intrigued to watch the dining guests as they arrive. It can be no easy thing to turn up to a pub alone on Christmas Day, announcing that you are here for the food, the free food, but the volunteers – each of them now with at least one unit of alcohol inside them – are full of unforced jollity. Ice is broken with enviable effortlessness. They know what they are doing. As the diners begin to appear, mostly one by one, occasionally in twos, the volunteers welcome them, offer them a drink, and then introduce them to their fellow diners. The moment the congregation has swelled to four, the quartet are redirected to a table filled with crackers, and the food begins to arrive: a salmon starter, turkey with all the trimmings to follow, and Christmas pudding at some point after that.

The majority of the guests – and today's guests will be closer to 50 than 500 – appear eager to talk. To eavesdrop on their individual conversations would be rude, and so I mostly don't, but what I do register is the constant hum of easy chit-chat between some very disparate people, the majority of them men, all of whom were strangers not five minutes previously. It's like a scene out of Dickens, the vulnerable finding solace and good cheer among one another in what must surely be the very definition of seasonal goodwill.

After he has pushed aside his starter ('I'm not keen on salmon'), one of the diners takes me aside. He is happy to talk, he says, and wants to know whether I would like to record the conversation. He won't give me his real name, he says, so I'll call him Morton. Morton is dressed in a faded, un-ironed three-piece suit. He is small and wizened, slightly stooped, his shoulders folded forwards, his head held back. He wears large laboratory-style glasses through which small eyes eagerly peer. I like him immediately. He tells me he is 74 years old, originally from Norway. He lived in the US for decades before settling in the UK in the late 1990s. He is a former university lecturer currently at work on a thesis that might, at some point, become a book. He says that he normally cooks for a close friend on Christmas Day at his central London flat, but that his friend has gone away this year, to visit family.

'So I'm all alone. I'm not lonely, though. Not that.'

So why, I ask, is he here?

He answers that he likes to cycle, and that he likes new destinations. A city empty of all traffic is too tempting a proposition for a cyclist not to take full advantage of. So he was always going to ride somewhere on Christmas Day. 'And the prospect of a free meal at the end of it appealed,' he says, his eyes glinting. It took him just over an hour to cycle the nine miles. I remember that he is 74. He must be exhausted, I suggest?

'Not at all,' he corrects. 'I feel perfectly fine.'

When the main course comes, he takes his plate to another table, and places his bag on the seat opposite. 'I prefer to eat alone,' he tells the volunteers who try to introduce further diners to his table. He waves me away, so that he can eat in peace. Later, he beckons me over again. He is fascinated by what he is seeing, he says. 'Who are these people who have turned up today? Do you know? They seem very friendly with one another. Have they met before?'

He thinks that the generosity of spirit on display is interesting, especially in the current climate. Nodding mostly to himself, he says: 'This might just be suggestive of a societal shift. Rather gives one renewed faith in the human race.'

There are all sorts of reasons, in any decade, to lose faith in the human race. This decade, it seems we've had even more reason to lose faith: in politics, in leadership, in consumerism run rampant. In the problem with men in general, as highlighted by the Time's Up and #MeToo campaigns. But as Morton might readily concur, all you need do is look around you to be reminded that the human race still beats with a very human heart. The way we are living life today is changing fast. It is within that change that so much has been lost, but not entirely. So many individuals are working hard now to reclaim it. It is when they come together to do this as a movement that it becomes most visible. As our awareness of isolation grows, there are now entire cities mobilising its people to come together to fight against it, to reconnect. This is how faith is restored.

Take, for example, Vancouver. Vancouver is often described as the ideal modern city. Sitting high up on the far west corner of Canada, perched above Seattle like a bird peering over a cliff, it is a city that enjoys its reputation, and actively courts it. Ask a typical Vancouverite – if there is such a thing (and for the purposes of this chapter there is, and he is a director at an architect firm by the name of Mark Busse) – to talk about his city, and he will tell you, as he told me, that Vancouver is indeed sleek and modern and urban, with ready access to natural splendour. It's the kind of place everyone would choose to live, if choice were made available. The city is on track to become the greenest on the planet, and it works hard to be as pluralistic, open, accessible, inclusive and progressive as it possibly can be. It fosters an environment of almost foreboding excellence, a place where productivity and innovation sit alongside environmental issues, each taken as seriously as the next at both governmental and societal level. Yes, it rains a lot, but there are umbrella shops.

But something interesting is happening to Vancouver that was never in the script, and it's making them uncomfortable. Vancouverites, Mark Busse tells me, have something of a reputation that has long been fostered, but rarely admitted to. 'It's true that we can come across as somewhat aloof, unfriendly,' he says. In a metropolis that is becoming increasingly multicultural, being aloof and unfriendly does not play well to the very notion of inclusiveness. Concern grew to the point where the city could no longer look at itself in the mirror for fear of what it might see staring back.

The local government decided to take a poll of its inhabitants. They wanted to know what pleased them about their city, but also what distressed them. Were there any prevailing issues they wanted dealt with? And what, if anything, could the city itself do to help?

The results of the poll, when digested over gluten-free breakfasts in organic cafés, made for queasy reading. It identified that its overriding issue was a severe case of collective loneliness. People were feeling increasingly socially isolated from one another, had become strangers living among strangers. The avoidance of eye contact had become the norm. People no longer knew their neighbours, and were feeling increasingly detached from their friends. Even office life had come to feel closed off, hemmed in, hermetically sealed. The poll had asked if people believed a neighbour might help them out in an emergency; if they felt part of a wider support network. The answer, in both cases, was no. The people no longer felt they had an audible voice in the city.

Vancouver's utopian ideal was duly scuppered. The local media had a field day.

'Everyone started pointing fingers,' says Mark Busse. 'Who was at fault? I think it came down to fear. There was a lot of fear. What had happened to our city? How could we bring it back?'

Those who might have convinced themselves the results were little more than hyperbole and exaggeration were soon silenced. The voices of discontent grew louder. A South African dweller in the city, speaking to *The Guardian*,[10] which was doing a piece on the lack of connectedness in cities, suggested that

Vancouver compared badly to the other six countries across four continents he had previously lived in. 'People don't call you back, they don't invite you out, they don't make eye contact,' he told the paper. The rain, he went on to suggest, didn't help.

And so the city, in the grip of an even greater self-consciousness, decided to act. In 2015, its City Hall set up Engaged City Task Force, a series of initiatives designed to make the metropolis more dynamic, more engaging and ultimately more liveable. 'It was about encouraging us all to form communities, and a kinship that would make society function in a better, healthier way,' Busse says.

Elsewhere, a project began, called Say Hello, which required willing individuals to wear badges that identify themselves as keen to talk. These slightly happy-clappy badge-wearers would then sit, somewhat ostentatiously, in public places, waiting for people to approach them, a convivial greeting on their lips.

'Sounds awful,' I say to Mark Busse. 'Did it work?' He laughs. 'Fat chance! But no, that's not important. What is important is that the intent was there. People really do want to have conversations with one another, they just don't want to be spoken down to in the process. They – we – just want to feel that we belong, that's all.'

Nevertheless, the badge initiative, a cute enough idea on paper, was subsequently replicated across the world, including in the UK. These British badges read I Talk to Strangers, and were made available in cafés and public spaces. One morning, Jessica Pan, a Texan living in London, came across one. She picked it up.

'I found the whole concept of talking to strangers rather strange and scary, but I took the badge anyway,' says Jessica. She was intrigued, she adds, because she had recently left her office job to become a freelance writer. 'And so I didn't see anybody anymore. I began to feel lonely, and then borderline depressed about it. I thought it was all very strange in London: there are millions of us here, and no one talks to anyone.'

Jessica was keen to reconnect. In Amarillo, where she was raised, people talked to one another all the time. Silence in a public place was unheard-of. There was always much to talk about! So why not talk?

'I knew, of course, that London is a notoriously cold city, but I didn't enjoy feeling isolated and cut off from the world simply because I work from home, so I thought to myself: what am I going to do about it?'

In the short term, Jessica, who is 32, took the badge. Eventually, she wore the badge. Regrettably, she soon forgot she was wearing it, which led to encounters that made her seem every bit as cold as any other Londoner.

'A man came up to me on a bridge one day and said to me, "I do, too." I backed away from him, so he repeated it: "I do, too."' Jessica was confused. She had no idea what he was talking about. A crazy person. 'And then he said: "Oh, it's not true. You don't." And he walked away.' It was only later that she realised he was referring to the badge that still sat unobtrusively on her coat's lapel. 'I felt terrible! Here I was rejecting a stranger who was only trying to do what I was suggesting I do.'

The experience made her come to a conclusion. 'Don't wear that badge! Because if you do, you are literally saying to the world: I am crazy! And nobody wants to talk to crazy people. I like the idea, I just don't think they work in practice. It puts people on their guard, and it makes you, the wearer, stand out, but in a bad way.'

The exercise nevertheless planted a seed somewhere deep inside Jessica. Talking to strangers needn't be that hard. It might even be beneficial. You might make friends. And so now, when the moment is right, when the context is right, she does just that. She talks to strangers.

'It makes you feel more human to connect with other people,' she says. 'You don't have to talk politics, or climate change. But now, when I walk into my local café, I just say "Hi, how's your day?" And they say "Hi" back. If you've not been feeling particularly great that day, it means a lot. It's just nice to feel that connection.'

Connection, in italics, is now the challenge of all modern cities: how to effect it? Vancouver has begun to target its urban planners, individuals like Mark Busse himself. Densification tends to happen at the expense of urban dwellers, and so greater effort is required. 'All cities have to cluster, of course, but we end up doing so on an individual basis,' he explains. 'And the more we cluster, the more isolated we feel. But that's because we are building a lot of ill-conceived, poorly constructed buildings and domiciles. That has to change.'

Like Jessica Pan, Mark Busse no longer wears his badge, but it did also leave its mark on him, this need to reconnect.

The architecture firm where he works as a designer and strategist now opens its doors once a month to other architecture firms, where they gather together, shooting the breeze over coffee and sharing ideas. They host public art events in their offices, and community conversation initiatives with an aim to transform downtown alleys into vibrant, active public spaces.

'And you know what? It works, being friendly. I now reach out to many more people myself as a result. And, okay, yes, perhaps some people might occasionally look at me as if I am crazy, but I'm fine with that. I can handle it. I mean, maybe I am crazy?'

Vancouver hasn't yet re-polled its citizens to gauge whether its efforts have been effective, but Mark Busse assures me that it will do. In the meantime, urban planners and architects the world over are now undertaking business trips to the city to see first-hand what they are doing, how they are doing it, and how the rest of us might attempt similar.

'We've won a major award for our initiatives,' he says, not without pride.

If their efforts are working, he goes on to suggest, it's because Canada has always been a left of centre kind of country.

That really helps, trust me, because nobody does fluffy better than the progressive left, right? The far right will think this all nonsense, of course. *Suck it up, pull up your big boy pants!*, they may well tell us. What we are doing here in Vancouver is prompting empathy on a wider scale. We are listening to the people, noting their concerns. It's a start.

Residents in Amsterdam, meanwhile, are trying to reconnect with their communities in more tangibly manageable ways. A recent initiative there encourages people in any kind of need to sign up to an online group. If, for example, you require a drill, don't go and buy one, but rather borrow it from your neighbour. It's not only entirely likely that one of your neighbours will have a drill, it's likely you've never met them before. This is one way to extend your social connections, and save money. There are countless similar initiatives springing up all over the world. All each of them needs is mass take-up. To go back to the South African quoted in *The Guardian* who had attempted to talk to people in his adopted Canadian city by wearing a Say Hello badge: 'Most people just keep to themselves. I was surprised at how little progress it made. People are just so shy, they are just so damn shy.'

However, the South African might be wrong here. Most of us aren't shy at all, not really. What most of us are ultimately after is an excuse, a reason, to start a conversation in a world that increasingly denies those excuses to us. We do want to step out of our bubbles, and extend a hand. Each of us is waiting for that domino to fall, the Say Hello badge to topple into the I Talk to Strangers badge, which topples into the community sharing initiative, the sudden impulse to call upon our elderly neighbours to see if they are okay, to express empathy better with our fellow students, our fellow parents, and colleagues, to the disabled, to refugees, to those at the beginning of life and those at the end.

And so on.

In Vancouver, I talk to city councillor Andrea Reimer, who tells me that, as much as representatives from countries around the world continue to flock to Vancouver to learn from their initiatives, she continues to look across the globe for similar stories of city inclusiveness initiatives. 'We want to learn more.' She is impressed by comparable undertakings in Brazil and Colombia, Malaysia and Singapore. Germany's decision in 2016 to open its borders to immigrants, she tells me, was a lesson to us all.

> This is all a massive challenge, but it's working, and here's why: each relationship we make is like a tree. Once that seed is embedded, it grows not into a single stalk but out into many different branches. Two people will become friends with 10; those 10 might become friends with hundreds more. And so, in time, we could well foster many thousands of new connections, new relationships. It's not linear, it will take time, and there will be setbacks. But we absolutely have to make the effort, for the simple reason that it's worth it.

In the time since her murder, Jo Cox's sister Kim Leadbeater has seen her life changed beyond recognition. Her mourning has been a curiously, perhaps unavoidably, public one, and one informed by a multiplicity of random acts of kindness, either directed specifically towards her and her family, or in Jo's honour. By dint of her work as a Member of Parliament, Jo had been used to the occasional glare of the public eye. But Kim was not.

Kim Leadbeater and her sister Jo grew up in a small Yorkshire town surrounded by familiar faces and the concrete notion of community. They were lucky in this, Kim says.

> We were happy. We had a happy upbringing. And we wanted others to be happy, too. We were brought up by our parents to

care about other people, about never seeing gender, colour, race or age, and so we never did. We never saw the differences in people, we just saw the people themselves.

Being raised in such a way, she believes, enabled them both to feel capable of reaching out to others, to stop and talk to anyone who might seem in need or distress. These made up countless acts of everyday kindness. But their determination to be good was compounded by a voluminous personality. Neither Kim nor her sister was the shy and retiring type. As I speak to Kim, I am put in mind of a bull in a china shop, one that knocks nothing off the shelves but leaves an indelible presence behind her nevertheless. She's a natural energy source. I first saw her at a conference on kindness in late 2017, where she had been booked to give a speech on her sister's legacy. Unlike Jo, Kim was not used to public speaking. Back home in Yorkshire, she is a personal trainer and life coach, and you have to figure she's a pretty effective one. She started her speech by telling us that she was a fish out of water here, terrified at the very idea of public speaking, that she didn't know what she was going to say and was sure she was about to fluff her lines. We were to forgive her in advance, she instructed.

In cleverly lowering our expectations of her, she then went on to give the most commanding, and entertaining, talk of the day. She came across like an exclamation mark made flesh. You wanted to stand up when she had finished talking and punch the air in admiration, even if you are not the type to punch the air. But then Kim revels in her ability at plain speaking, telling it like it is. This, she will tell you, is Yorkshire grit. If she is a woman with ambiguities, then she hides them well. To the untrained eye, she is purely indomitable.

During her talk, she told us about how coming down to London always bewildered her, about how all of us city dwellers, when out and about, walked with our chins nestled into our scarves, which themselves were nestled deep within our coats until we were hunched over into ourselves and lost to the world around us. Where was the friendliness in that? The inclusivity? The approachability she was used to seeing back home in Yorkshire? Kim wanted to stop all the commuters in their tracks, she told us, to say hello to them the way others might cry for help (i.e., loudly), and even to hug a few, if she felt the sudden urge to do so. 'I warn you now,' she said from the podium, 'I'm a hugger.'

In the past, for Kim trips to London were always fleeting affairs, mostly to see her sister, her brother-in-law, her growing nephew and niece. Since Jo's death, her visits have increased but for very different reasons. Here, she has been working more in her late sister's stead, adamant that Jo's message reaches as many people as possible, and that as many people as possible then act upon it. She wants to ensure that the surfeit of goodwill that instinctively materialised in the immediate aftermath of her death doesn't just linger but endures. She wants it to outlast the newscycle.

At first, I'll be honest with you, we just wanted to ensure that our own community wasn't completely fractured by Jo's murder, because at the beginning that did seem like a very frightening possibility. So we worked hard to bring the different communities together, to work alongside one another, and to actually get to know each other, to become friends.

It worked, she says, insistently. Then, along with the Foundation and The Eden Project, which works to promote resilience and sustainability in the modern world, they launched The Great Get Together, a project that essentially promoted community spirit on a national level. On the weekend of the first anniversary of Jo's death, 9.3 million people did just that, up and down the UK. There was bunting, and an awful lot of gingham.

The momentum has been gathering ever since. In Yorkshire, 800 children from 23 local schools came together to walk through Batley beneath banners reading More in Common. Joggers have organised charity runs; people have run the marathon in Jo's name. There has been a mass bike ride from Spen to Parliament to trace Jo's career in politics. Local Muslims were introduced to the British religion of rugby on a Sunday. At one match Kim attended, she sat next to an Imam. 'He didn't have a clue what was going on, but he loved it,' she says, adding:

And we just keep hearing all sorts of stories of people coming together, neighbours who had never met one another before, and different cultures that they perhaps hadn't associated with and might even have gone out of their way to avoid. But they met up, they got together, they became friends. And that's been amazing to witness. I'm sad, of course, that it required a tragedy to bring out the best in people, but tragedy does have a habit of doing that.

When we speak, Kim is approaching her eighteenth relentless month of community work, but in many ways, she suggests, her work is just beginning.

I'm under no illusion. I'm aware that a lot of the work we've done so far has been preaching to the converted, but progress really has been made, and that's the most encouraging thing, I think. We've made such a lot of progress, barriers have been broken down, friendships forged. But the effort is ongoing.

In the weeks after we speak, her work continuing to gather momentum, the government appoints the MP Tracey Crouch as its 'Minister for Loneliness'. There has never been a Minister for Loneliness before, and so this represents a seismic shift, proof indeed that the pressure is being felt, heard, listened to.

This, says Kim, is good news. It means that the subject is at last on the table, a definable thing, no longer amorphous but tangible, its stigma lifted. Now the proper work can begin.

I talk to Tracey Crouch in the weeks after her appointment. In addition to being the first Minister for Loneliness, the Conservative MP is also the Minister for Sport and Civil Society, so she's juggling several plates. They complement one another, she tells me, and explains that she is nothing if not realistic about her new position.

'Oh, it's an enormous challenge,' she freely admits, 'but ever since the announcement I've just been met with overwhelming positivity everywhere I go. I think that's a reflection of the work Jo did, that this is a subject about working together, and it's a reminder that sometimes there are issues that are not party political.'

The enormous challenges are not hers alone, of course, but on the question of what precisely government itself can do, she suggests that, in fact, it can do plenty. 'We can lead the conversation, we can act as policy leaders, and we can help with coordination and facilitation. But you're right,' she concedes, 'everybody has to play a role here, because it's an issue that affects everybody. It's not one of those issues where it's just about central government and their efforts, but about local government too, about community organisations and individuals themselves, the role every one of us has to play in our own neighbourhoods. But I do believe that local government, especially, will be a key partner in all this. We need to be aware of the unintended consequences that certain policy developments might leave behind them.'

She talks about rural communities. If a local authority axes one of its bus services, then an unintended consequence could be that it leaves people feeling more cut off from their villages and communities. Likewise the closing of local pubs and post offices. It will inevitably take far more than the threat of mere loneliness to make a bus company think twice about cancelling a route if it is no longer financially viable to do so, but the MP insists that these will be issues to look at more closely from now on. Every decision has a consequence. What are those consequences, and how might they affect people's lives negatively?

She points to other efforts, including those in sport, where people are working to tackle the issue. Blackburn Rovers has recently addressed the problems of isolation in its own community by bringing it together under the banner of football, and has done so successfully. She talks about increasing the understanding of working with the disabled and the elderly, along with the mental health benefits of interacting not just with fellow human beings but also with animals.

'We're currently doing a lot of work with animal welfare societies, because animals are an amazing way of providing companionship for people. So rather than prescribing pills, we'd much rather prescribe community activities that everyone can get involved with, and everyone can benefit from.'

Politicians are routinely held to account over their effectiveness or, in many cases, distinct lack of. A soundbite only lasts as long as the breath that was required to utter it; but what's behind it? To this end, Tracey Crouch is already fielding questions over her efforts to date. In other words, is it working?

She smiles. 'I can tell you that I won't be the Minister that finally sees an end to this condition. This will take a generation to change, and I, personally, am not going to eradicate loneliness during the course of my appointment. No, what we are undertaking here is a much longer-term project, and one in which all of us have to play our part if we are to ensure, in the future, that people have a better understanding of the issue, and also more effective solutions. It takes a long time to address stigma – look how long it took before we started to have proper conversations about mental health – but we have started this with loneliness now, we are addressing it, and so change will happen. It won't happen overnight. And it won't be a case of government simply pumping money into it, either – though I do hope that we will have innovation funds and financial opportunities and so on – but instead about all of us working together. Already I've seen so many amazing projects and initiatives; I've seen the best of people, some really incredibly dedicated people, paid and unpaid, and I've been witness to projects that go well beyond the norm. It's been encouraging.'

The emails arrive into the Jo Cox Foundation on a daily basis, much as they have been doing since September 2016. They murmur onto laptops with an arriving chime, always unbidden, always welcome, and they come first thing in the morning, last thing at night, over the weekend. They are sent from individuals, mostly, people in towns and cities and villages inspired by what they have seen on television and read in the media, and have felt motivated to attempt something similar themselves. Letters come, too, on paper, on Basildon Bond, often including donations that the Foundation never requested but, as any charity would, very gratefully receive. The Foundation's director, Iona Lawrence, says it is always a humbling experience.

Somebody sent a cheque for £3 recently, with an apology that it wasn't very much. But if everybody keeps sending in cheques for £3, it all adds up to something very meaningful indeed. It seems that everybody wants to play their part, individuals finding their own purpose, doing more in their places of work, or at home, their local communities. They don't need our permission, they just go ahead and do something: they have get-togethers of their own, they raise money, and they send it through to us. I have to tell you that the amount of goodwill on display has been heart-warming. It's been an incredible wave to ride.

These letters of goodwill pile up on their desks every day, and every day Iona and her colleague Lily Piachaud sift through them, increasingly aware that, taken individually, they are little more than whispers, but that collectively, they are becoming a roar.

One letter reads:

Please find enclosed cheques to the value of £30. After seeing your latest TV campaign, Mince Pie Moments, I thought it would be a lovely idea to invite neighbours round for a pie and a cuppa. We live in a very small street and lots of us have been here for 15 years, but generally only say hello. Our street is now quite multicultural, and I only had a few people come, but small steps. I'm hoping to build on this to have a coffee morning once a month. I know the amount raised isn't much, but I hope you can put it to good use.

Mince Pie Moments was one of the Foundation's pre-Christmas initiatives in 2017 that encouraged people to get together over something festive with a high calorific content.

Another letter reads:

To the Jo Cox charity,

   My mother recently passed away and as her only daughter I chose the Jo Cox
Charity to benefit from the retiring collection at the crematorium. Mum was
nearly 95 and like myself was a member of The Women's Institute, and at our
Annual Conference in June this year one of the resolutions that was passed was
about alleviating loneliness. I know that this was a cause dear to Jo's heart who
like myself was a West Yorkshire girl.

The Jo Cox Foundation was originally set up to represent
three of Jo's keenest interests – the White Helmets, which
offer civilian protection in Syria; The Royal Voluntary
Service, which works with older people and communities;
and Hope Not Hate, which brings fractured communities
together – but has now branched out into so many other
areas. It works with MPs and individuals alike, and if Jo's
sister Kim has occasionally felt that, right now at least, they
are merely preaching to the converted, this gradual take-up
on a national level, alongside the government's appointment
of a loneliness minister, surely suggests that the converted
are growing in numbers. Iona Lawrence tells me that she
is constantly amazed by what people do, the actions they
take, which are every bit as important as the donations they
offer. 'We are overwhelmed and hugely grateful for people's
donations,' she says, 'they are an important way for people
to act, but we also hugely value the actions people take:
the lunch clubs, the coffee mornings and other community
things they do.'

All these actions are part of the domino effect. The more people act, the more other people feel moved to do likewise.

In the wake of Tracey Crouch's appointment, there were newspaper columns as far afield as Brazil, Germany and India, in which columnists wondered whether their countries should start taking more affirmative action to address their own problems around social isolation. Whether such effort will be proved ultimately effective, from a scientific perspective, and whether it will succeed in reducing the dangers (on a par with smoking, remember) for those it afflicts, inevitably remains to be seen, and no doubt interested parties – all those psychologists and sociologists so fascinated by how modern life shall affect us long-term – will devote a great part of their studies to this work in time.

But we can only lay future foundations by addressing the here and now, and right now we are at the beginning still. A great many of us are congregating at its starting line, and, much as one person yawning makes the next person yawn, the more we see one another inspired by the Foundation, the more we will all be prompted into affirmative action. Incipiently, the clamour is becoming a din. It's in the media all the time these days, and so at last loneliness has snagged its headline status. The world is sitting up, taking notice.

And at least one effect *is* immediate. We are all aware of loneliness now. We recognise it more, in ourselves, in those we love, in those we don't yet know particularly well. We are starting to know whom to approach for help, and accepting that asking for help isn't a failing. It's what makes us human, a community, people. Gradually, we are learning to help ourselves help ourselves.

The aim of this book has been, simply, to continue the conversation Jo Cox had started. The conversation is ongoing. Join it.

References

1. Introduction. Campaign to End Loneliness, 'Lonely visits to the GP'.
2. Introduction. British Red Cross, 'Isolation and Loneliness'.
3. Introduction. 'Three quarters of old people in the UK are lonely, survey finds', *The Guardian*, 21 March, 2017.
4. Introduction. The Jo Cox Commission on Loneliness, *Addressing loneliness in disabled people*. 2017.
5. Introduction. 'All the lonely people', *The New York Times*, 18 May, 2013.
6. Introduction. 'Millennials shun face-to-face conversations in favour of social media and online messaging', *The Independent*, 29 January, 2018.
7. Chapter 1. *Loneliness: Human Nature and the Need for Social Connection*, John T. Cacioppo & William Patrick, Norton, 2009.
8. Chapter 1. 'Loneliness as harmful as smoking, says Jo Cox Commission', *The Times*, 15 December, 2017.
9. Chapter 8. *IGen: Why Today's Super-Kids Are Growing up Less Rebellious, More Tolerant, Less Happy – And Completely Unprepared for Adulthood – and What That Means for the Rest of Us*, Jean M. Twenge, Atria Books, 2017.
10. Chapter 13. 'Is Vancouver lonelier than most cities or just better about addressing it?', *The Guardian*, 4 April, 2017.

Acknowledgements

I would like to thank everybody who took the time to talk to me, to tell me about their work and their often very personal situations, and how they are working together to make everybody, all of us, less lonely, less isolated and more connected. I'm particularly grateful to Iona Lawrence, Alexia Latham, Julianne Marriott, Steve Cole, Hannah Morrish, Jade Gadd, Mark Busse, Dr Ron Roberts, Diana Saif, Melissa Rose Lawrence, Lily Piachaud, Ian Treherne, Sara Maitland, Michelle Kennedy, Dawn Cahill and Ali Somers. Thank you to Kim Leadbeater, for being an inspiration. To Tracey Crouch MP, for taking up the cause. To Sarah Skipper for attention to detail. And to Charlotte Croft for everything else, and everything in between.

About the author

Nick Duerden is a writer and journalist. He has written for newspapers and magazines in the UK and US on topics including the arts, health, travel and family. His memoir, *Get Well Soon* (Bloomsbury), is about a long period of ill-health that proved NHS-resistant, forcing him to delve into the world of alternative therapy in pursuit of a cure.

Index